TRAVELS WITH A BIKE

Published by
Impression Publishing
www.impressionpublishing.net

All rights reserved.

No part of this book may be reproduced in any form by photocopying or any electronic or mechanical means, including information storage or retrieval systems, without permissions in writing from both the copyright owner and the publisher of the book.

First Edition published 2012
© John Brown 2012

Printed and bound in Great Britain by
printmyownbook.com

A catalogue record for this book
is available from The British Library
ISBN 978-1-908374-56-1

TRAVELS WITH A BIKE

Forward: By John Brown

I first met Irene *one Enchanted Evening* at the Kursaal dance rooms, Southend on sea. It was New Year's Eve 1952 and South Pacific was showing at the local Cinema. I saw Irene *'across a crowded room'* she was 19, I was 24. I thought her so beautiful.

Irene in 1952

I asked her to dance, and later when the balloons floated down to bring in 1952 we kissed for the first time and we knew from that moment that our destiny lay together. I was very adventurous and loved the outdoors, and wanted to share with Irene places in Europe that I had first visited when I was in the army. So (with the permission of her very Methodist parents) we planned our trip. It was to be on two bikes (no gears) with two sets of panniers and £25 each to last as long as possible. That was in 1952.

I often wonder if our 3 months of hardship, hunger and deprivation, prepared us for life's journey and cemented our 60 years of love.

This is the diary I kept during our travels, printed exactly as I wrote it back in 1952.

TRAVELS WITH A BIKE

Irene and I

Arrival in Belgium - August 1952

Sailed from Dover on a boat for Ostende. It was more like a Southend tripper outing than anything else, although there were a good few hikers and school parties aboard. All kit had to be removed from our cycles before loading, and we had quite a hectic time getting through both lots of customs. At Ostende we joined up with four others and cycled the fifteen miles to Brugge in fine time. The road was perfectly flat and the going extremely easy.

Just inside Brugge, the spindle on Irene's back wheel tightened up so that the wheel wouldn't go round. The back wheel, plus all the kit, had to come off in order to fix it. I was not very pleased. Eventually we reached the youth Hostel at seven.

Money troubles started at once. Two francs for fifteen minutes gas. It was just enough for a cup of tea and some baked beans, still we were satisfied. Walked around the town. It's a quaint old place, bells seem to be ringing all the time. I think Brugge would be best visited in the winter when there are less tourists. After seeing the various prices of goods in the shops we decided to go to Holland as soon as possible.

12 August 1952 Tuesday

Ate bread and jam for breakfast at the hostel and then headed for Sluis, 10 miles away on the Dutch border. Crossed the border with little difficulty about 11 am. The land was quite flat and we cycled along easily with no hitches.

Stopped by some pear trees for a midday snack. The pears were hard but edible. The countryside was far more inhabited than we had expected. Agriculture was very intense and we could not have found a decent camp site even if we had wanted one.

Irene was impressed by the cleanliness and orderliness of everything. The houses especially were brightly painted, small and very neat. Often they had bright flower boxes at the windows and over the door. The main crops seemed to be oats, flax and kale. Pear trees were by far the most abundant of the fruit trees.

After lunch we cycled through several sleepy little towns. The biggest of these being Oostburg. The weather was variable, sometimes hot and sunny, and then cloudy and windy. We stayed for about two hours resting by the road at a spot not far from Biervliet. Ate more bread and jam there and also slept a little. The road surfaces became really bad. We were right off the beaten track and were forced to rattle for miles over cobbles. Irene's arm was aching but she didn't complain. Reached the canal connecting Turneuzen and Ghent. That really is a canal. Far larger than any we have seen in England. The place seemed more industrial and some of the barges were 100 yards long. They were mostly laden with coal or straw, and came from as far away as Strasbourg.

In the town of Axel, after some difficulty in making ourselves understood, a policeman very kindly took us a mile to the hostel. The warden and his wife greeted us well and shook hands. The hostel is new, quite large, and seemed to have every amenity. It was by far the best one we have seen. Meals were cheap so we had them supplied ready cooked by the warden. For supper I have never tasted such a delicious mixture as they made out of potatoes, lettuce, hot beetroot and apple sauce. We both felt completely satisfied. I think the gravy was the secret of it.

There were two other English people there and several Dutch and Belgians. Most of them spoke our language so we had no difficulty. Everyone was very friendly. I think this was due really to the warden and his wife. They were such pleasant people. We spent the evening playing party games and listening to the piano.

13 August 1952 Wednesday

Hostel duties were washing up and sweeping the dormitories. Then we left in good spirits about 8.30. Soon came to the town of Hulst. Walked around a bit and bought some meat. We wanted to get a good meal before going back into Belgium where food is too expensive. Tried one spot to cook a meal, but it smelt bad and was too wet. So we moved on and crossed the frontier. Found a pleasant spot just off the road, so stopped and cooked a good meal. Then went to sleep for four hours off and on. I think this unusual method of living is proving rather tiring for us for a day or so until we get used to it.

Irene and I had the first of the many little tiffs, always they are due to my impatience and her slowness. We are both to blame. This time she didn't want to move off in a hurry, and I shouted at her, she burst into tears, and we made it all up beautifully Her arm is rather painful at times and I feel sorry for her. She is bearing up remarkably well on the whole.

Cycled pretty steadily to the outskirts of Antwerp, then stopped by the road and ate tea. Also changed into warmer clothes as it was getting chilly.

Had to go through a tunnel to get into the town. It was difficult getting the bikes down the moving stairs. Irene managed the first flight and then gave up, so I carried out a sort of shuttle service. Just as I was nearing the top of the last flight someone stopped the stairs, and this meant lugging the bike the rest of the way up.

It must have been about seven when we entered Antwerp. Plenty of people, neon lights and cafes. The whole place had a wonderful atmosphere of being 'alive' (for those with money, how we regretted then our lack of it.) Bought two lovely bags of chips and sat on a wall opposite the central station eating them.

It was growing dark and we had to find a place to camp, so we left Antwerp and set out on the road to Holland. The prospect of finding a site didn't look too good as everywhere was built up. Met two Dutch artists who had hitch-hiked from Monte Carlo. They lived in The Hague and were flat broke. Offered to lend them money, but they thought they would try and manage without it.

Took a side turning, and after much groping around in the dark, managed to conceal ourselves snugly in some bushes. It started to rain!

14 August 1952 Thursday

Some time in the early hours I got up and fixed the tent. The rain made groping around in the wet bushes rather a messy business. Still the tent gave protection from the rain and we slept fitfully till daybreak. The rain stopped and we had a quick wipe round with a wet flannel by way of a wash, and were away on the road by seven.

Halfway through Mariaburg a huge Alsation dog chasing a smaller one, crashed smack into Irene and knocked her over. She was very shaken and had a large bruise on the ankle, besides giving the shoulder another jolt. The people nearby were very kind. Phoned for the doctor, and brought a glass of soda water and a chair. Then we were invited into a house to wait for the doctor to arrive. He took us back to the surgery and gave an injection to stop the ankle paining until we could reach the hostel at Bergen op Zoom.

The doctor could not speak English, but was very nice. Took us back to the house we had waited in, and cut his fee from 150 to 80 francs when he saw that was all we had, even though we offered to make up the difference in Dutch Guilders..

We were given an excellent breakfast and talked for some time. Thought they were being extremely kind, then found out it was their dog that had caused the crash! The ride to Bergen op Zoom was uncomfortable, but we got there by about 1 pm.

Pitched the tent in the hostel grounds and left Irene to rest while I went shopping. The food was extremely cheap so I was most pleased. The hostel had not the same atmosphere as Axel and we didn't have much to do with it. The warden told us we could only stay one night, so I did not feel too friendly towards him then. There was no need for it as we were only camping in a huge field. Irene slept in the hostel and I in the tent.

15 August 1952 Friday

Irene came over from the hostel and woke me. I had slept soundly all night. She got into my bed and went to sleep again. I got breakfast. Afterwards I spent three hours looking around for a new place to camp. A site known as De Kloof would not take us as we were man and woman. Finally found a small house in a field. The man said we could move there.

Went back to the hostel and packed our kit. Then had a good fry up for dinner and finished off with an apple suet pudding. It tasted excellent.

Moved to the new camp site and just got the tent pitched when a terrific thunderstorm started. We were invited into the little house, and the owner helped us to quickly move all the kit. It was a good thing as the tent leaked terribly. Still it would take a mighty strong tent to stand up to that storm. There were hail stones as big as glass marbles.

The family who took us in were named Van Loom. They consisted of the father and Mother, aged 25, Father 33, and three children, two girls and a boy named Mindje, Ridje, and Ardre. They seemed a happy enough family but very poor. The man worked as some kind of miner. I could not quite understand more. It was a Catholic feast day, so he was not at work. They were ardent Catholics.

The house consisted of two sections. One end was more or less a barn. In there was a stove for the cooking. Also various stores were kept there beside a cluck of chickens and a dog named Neru. It was to be our sleeping chamber also, looked heavenly, after sitting for a while in that leaking tent. The other half of the house was a little less barbaric. One room about twenty feet square, was the bedroom and also best front parlour for the whole family. The other room was a small sort of dining room. There was also a room upstairs, but we didn't see that.

We had our meals with the family. Three eggs each, piles of bread and margarine, and some of the best coffee I have ever tasted. We spent the evening learning to speak Dutch, but I don't think we got far. Certainly felt thankful we were not camping. Lying in bed the sounds were very strange. Dog scratching, mice squeaking and a cluck of chicks making all the noises that a cluck of chicks make.

Irene on right with Van Loom family in Holland

16 August 1952 Saturday

Irene's arm was painful during the night, and she didn't feel too sure of the mice, so didn't sleep too well and it took her a long time to get going. I had been up, made the bed roll and taken the two little girls for a walk around the garden before she made it.

We had a good though simple breakfast, and then packed the kit and loaded it on the bikes. Took photos of the family, then gave them some tinned stuff and money and left. Spent an hour at the bank in Bergen op Zoom and got a cheque cashed. Then set out on the road to Breda.

First we intended to make for Amsterdam, then changed our minds for Rotterdam, and finally as we had not reached Breda by 2 in the afternoon, decided to stay at the hostel in Gineeken nearby.

Stopped for a bag of chips just outside Breda and then made for Gineeken and reached there by 2.45 so had to wait for the hostel to open. Both felt tired. Decided to stay three days at the hostel as Irene's various maladies needed resting.

Went out and spent some francs on bones for soup. Then had a good cook up. One of the few Dutch hostels that supplied self-cooking facilities. Also had a cold shower.

There is some festival on in the Breda district and everywhere we saw the 1252-1952 placards commemorating the 700th anniversary of the founding of the city. Oranges seemed to be the main emblem. Took a walk around Gineekin and looked at a fair ground. Everything seemed very cheerful.

Later did a lot of writing, then had tea (the Dutch variety, it's putrid!) and went to bed.

17 August 1952 Sunday

Bread and margarine with a bit of sugar for breakfast. We're getting short, must keep an eye on the budget.

Set out on foot for a day in Breda, but spent most of it either looking for a ladies' convenience, or somewhere to sit and rest. We both felt extremely tired.

Breda was highly decorated for the 700th year anniversary. Irene was surprised at the amount of activity even though it was Sunday.

Had a plate of chips and a glass of milk for dinner, then walked out into the country and picked blackberries. Also lay under a tree and slept for an hour or so. Returned to the hostel by three and cooked a good meal. Felt better then. Two English school boys who had hitch-hiked up the Rhine kept us amused. Spent the evening in the common room writing letters. Pleasant atmosphere.

Van Loom family

18 August 1952 Monday

Spent day cycling around in Breda, but Irene felt very tired and went to sleep on a seat. Later we went out into the country and ate our bread and marg. Youth Hostel for the night.

Had a jolly good meal of mashed potatoes all mixed up with bits of bacon (100 grams for 25 cents). Very pleasant in the kitchen with two Germans, a Scottish couple who had come from Barcelona, and a lad from Sweden. He advised us to go to Stockholm if we wanted work. Gave us the address of a hostel there.

19 August 1952 Tuesday

Started cycling to Amsterdam. Police directed us off the main road as it is forbidden for cyclists. Found ourselves on a cart track in the middle of a field. It started to rain, then Irene got a puncture. Mended it in a barn, watched by some very silent children.

Cycled on a bit and stopped under a bridge to shelter. The oldish Scottish couple from the hostel were there, and they made us tea on their primus. Also gave us a chocolate each which went down very well. This couple were in Holland for two weeks and spending a very enjoyable holiday touring on a tandem.

Managed to reach the town of Delft, and then discovered another puncture in Irene's back wheel. Had some sugar sandwiches and mended the puncture.

Went into Delft for a look around. We were just standing still sheltering from more rain, when Irene's tyre went down again. Had to buy a large patch for the tyre this time. A German asked us to watch his bike and gave us an apple each. An English tourist, proper cockney, asked for a ladies' place. We couldn't oblige and saw her ask a policeman.

Mended the puncture, went 100 yards and down it went again. Back to the old spot and tried to find the hole by putting the tyre through a puddle. Two buckets of water were brought out simultaneously. Couldn't find the hole so resigned myself to periodic pumping. Bought chips on the outskirts of Delft after listening to long and unintelligible directions for getting to Loosduinen. According to the various people we asked its distance was somewhere between 8 and 25 kilometres. We set out in a rather dejected mood.

However it seemed to be nearest town and we arrived at the huge hostel soaking wet and without food. Back down the road to the town for bread and eggs, and then a huge supper. Pleasant company there. The two young Scots from Barcelona. Bed very tired. The warden looked like Peter Ustinov.

20 August 1952 Wednesday

Left Loosduinen hostel about 9.30 after messing about for a long time with Irene's puncture. At last put a 27" tube in. It was given us by a Londoner just going home.

Drew some money at a bank in The Hague, then kept going steady for nearly two hours. Didn't think much of Holland's capital.

There was a head wind blowing which made cycling very difficult. Ate our dinner under a bridge. Bread and sugar, but Irene tried putting cocoa on the bread, and liked it. Changed our plans and instead of going to Amsterdam, headed to Haarlem as the weather was getting worse. Irene put trousers on, and halfway through the process she got very excited because I told her a whole party of bikers were coming along just outside Haarlem, Irene got another puncture. It really made me mad. Didn't take long to mend though.

Met two English girls in Haarlem and we all went to the Hostel together. Irene got in, but I couldn't, so decided to kip rough anywhere. Went out and did some shopping and had a good meal. Irene burnt the mince, but that's now a forbidden subject.

Spent evening mooching around. Talked to a Swiss boy. Met two college boys from London. Good fun they were. Made cocoa, and then managed to get a bed in the hostel, so everything turned out o.k. It was raining cats and dogs outside.

21 August 1952 Thursday

Had breakfast before 7, and left hostel about 8.30. Cycled steadily along a smooth cycle track all the way to Amsterdam. We were just approaching the Centrum when my handlebars snapped. This necessitated a new handlebar. Irene felt starving hungry as usual.

Tried a couple of shops and then got directions to the Westor Cycle Co. A man there spoke English and produced just what we needed. However he wanted 10 guilders. This rather took my breath away, and they must have taken pity on our plight. We were taken to a workshop and they put a good second-hand handlebar on for me. When I offered to pay they said it was nothing.

Then we picked a spot on the main road by a bridge, and I went and got some bread, cheese, tomatoes and plums. By this time we were just about famished, and had just started our meal when a lady came and made various signs for us to follow. So we did, and she led us to a pleasant seat in the gardens of the museum. It was kind of her, but actually we were quite happy where we were, we could have watched what was happening. Still I suppose the new spot was better really. After lunch we had an ice cream, Irene went to sleep and I tinkered with my bike. Cycled around Amsterdam, but decided it would be better in the country when you have no money. These Dutch towns have such tempting things to offer and we are always hungry.

Once out of the town we fairly ripped along for 20 miles to the town of Soest. Bought some food there and after a lot of looking around, found the hostel. Spent the usual sort of evening, although the hostellers we met this time seemed to be rather young and silly. We were the only English. Had a terrific stew for supper. Maybe we put too much salt in but otherwise it was fine. Finished up with cocoa and buiscuits.

22 August 1952 Friday

Hostel duties, potatoes for me, and pears for Irene. After that left feeling a bit downhearted over the loss of a guilder.

Cycled through Amersford and then Irene's bike had another puncture. That's about eight so far in that back wheel. Soon mended it o.k. and carried on towards Appeldoon. Ate lunch beside a field of potatoes. Then a man came along and gave us a pear each.

The countryside is getting a lot better, dryer and with more trees. We often managed to pick up fallen apples beside the road. Did some shopping in Appeldoon and were lucky to get a good bit of bacon quite cheap. The butcher also gave us a piece of sausage each to try. It was good. Kept going then through very pleasant country towards Deventer and we passed through it about 6 pm.

Now we were looking for a spot to cook our supper, and at last found one near a railway level crossing where we also got some water. It was in a small wood. I made the fire and Irene prepared the potatoes. We had a German dish called "Ein Topf". It consisted of bits of fried bacon mixed with potatoes and apples with sugar and salt.

Left to look for a camp site, but stopped in a small town to look around a fair. Typically German, the noise was deafening. A policeman shouted because Irene had no lights.

Made camp in a wood about 10pm. Then it was getting dusk. So we packed our kit, cycled two or three kilos up the road and then lay our bedding down in the middle of a pine wood and slept beneath the stars. Just a little scared as usual.

23 August 1952 Saturday

GERMANY

Woke at first light, beautiful morning, and the spot we had picked in the pines proved to be ok. We packed our kit and then moved just a short way up the road and made a fire and had breakfast. They were milking the cows in the fields so it must have been early. After that we made good progress through beautiful countryside and had a midday meal between Hengelo and Enschede. It was a good spot beside the road. The sun shone strongly. We both had a good tidy up and a wash as well. Spent seven guilders in Enschede buying up supplies before going to Germany. Also had a look around the market there and bought some plums.

A little way out of the town we crossed a small bridge, filled in a form, and were in Germany. Immediately the road worsened and everywhere looked slovenly. We noticed though that the people were better mannered than the Dutch. We cycled straight through Gronau and cooked our evening meal by a river. It wasn't a success, fish, too many bones for Irene, and I ate too much. A German motor cyclist stopped by and chatted for a long while. He was quite helpful.

24 August 1952 Sunday

Up and away very early. Cycled a good way and passed Burgsteinfurt. Saw nuns going two by two to church. By this time we were feeling the effect of our early rising. I think it was a mistake to cycle so far without breakfast. Pushed the bikes into a wood and had coffee and chocolate on bread. A family picking blackberries came and talked with us. After breakfast had a little clean up with a damp flannel, then cycled along the road to Lear. Passed for miles between apple trees growing on the roadside, also pears. Ate lots of fruit. Bought a huge loaf of dark coloured bread for 1 mark 40 pfennings. This rather shook us, but we thought afterwards it was good value as it was so large and heavy.

Started looking for a place to make dinner. We had decided on a big midday meal. Pealed the potatoes, then filled up the water bottles. This gave us more water to spare for the dinner. Turned off the road and went along a track past two or three farms, and made our fire by a path in a wood. It was very quiet and not too light. Had a large meal. Then Irene went to sleep and I had a go at making suet pudding. It was smoky and too sweet, so we had to throw it away.

Didn't leave the wood until 4 pm then we cycled the ten or twelve miles into Munster very fast. All the people were out taking their Sunday stroll when we arrived in Munster. Decided to stay at the Youth Hostel. The warden was out but we had a good wash, then tea. Took a walk around the town looking respectable for once. All the tank regiments were away on a scheme so we didn't see any of my pals. Went into the NAAFI club and spent our sixpences on tea, chips and cakes. It went down very well. Asked some young soldiers where all the lads were, but they didn't know. "We only came Tuesday," was the answer in a broad Brummy accent, they were looking most lost.

25 August 1952 Monday

Collected a letter from Mum at the Post Office. Irene was disappointed at not getting one also. The weather was not very bright, so we cycled at a good speed for 50 kilometres. Irene's back tyre blew out on the way and had to be changed. Yet we did the journey in less than three hours. Ended up by cooking a meal of black sausage in a wood just out of Wiedenbruck, then I went to sleep and Irene wrote a letter, then she went to sleep and I wrote one. Between us we dwindled away the whole afternoon and it was getting dusk when we moved out.

Decided to find a place to camp, but first washed the dixies in a canal, and had a bottle full of delicious milk given us free though I offered to pay. It was practically dark but we built a fire and made a delicious cup of cocoa all milk. It really was good.

Cycled on a bit and asked at a farm if we could sleep in a barn. They put a huge pile of straw down, gave us a fine lot of ham for supper, and then for two hours we watched a pig giving birth to eight babies. I wonder what will happen next.

26 August 1952 Tuesday

Slept very warm and snug in the straw and didn't get up until after 7. We were given tinned meat for breakfast and we ate a huge meal. Then Paul Lunning, (the English-speaking son) started playing the piano. So we went into the drawing room and spent an hour listening to him and his sister. I also had a go on the piano. Left about 9.30 with sandwiches packed and every good wish. Promised to write and perhaps come again one day.

Cycling seemed to be extremely hard work and we couldn't make much headway. Also the countryside was not very interesting. Posted our letters in Lipstatt and then went on to Erwitte. Felt just about tired out. A lorry gave us a lift for 15 miles to Warstein which cheered us up no end. It is in hilly country and a lot of quarrying goes on. Sat by a pond in the town and ate the sandwiches. A women in black spoke to us for quite a while even though we told her we couldn't understand. Left Warstein and were forced to walk up a hill. It was a complete optical illusion, looking forward the road seemed to be going down, not up. The hill kept on and on, at each bend we expected to see the summit, but there was another gentle slope just the same as the last. It was quite pleasant walking though. Pinewoods and sunshine, the scenery was beautiful before reaching the top. Then we had a lovely run downhill for a few miles right into Meschede.

Bought some food and an ice cream, then set out along the road to Brilon. The country still very hilly and we had to walk a good deal. We wanted to get to Winterberg so were directed up a turning to the right. This took us up through Ostig. From then our enquiries didn't bear much fruit. Nobody seemed to have heard of Winterberg. Still we pushed on. We were travelling on a rough track going up a valley. It was getting towards evening, so when we came to a fork in the road we decided to make the evening meal. It was a pleasant spot with a fast stream going under a bridge. We lit the fire on the bridge and ate egg and chips.

There was nobody about and we didn't get a chance to ask directions until a car pulled up. They were also lost, but told us a village was 4 kilometres along the fork to the right. They then went back the way they had come.

After our meal we started towards the village although we were looking for a spot to pitch the tent. The night was fine, but dewey and damp and we thought it best to have shelter if possible. Reached the village before seeing anything likely, and met again the people lost with the car. Had a little chat, they were on 8 days holiday and came from Hamm, had decided to spend the night at the inn.

Asked at a house the way to Winterberg, and was told. Then went to another house and asked to sleep in the barn. We had resolved to take nothing more as it seemed a bit much to accept German hospitality two nights on the run. However there was no help for it without being rude. We were treated extremely well to tea and cakes, and then spent an hour in the living room talking. They also put on the 10pm news from England for us. Slept on the floor in their living room. They were a family that seemed to have had a lot of trouble. One son aged 24 had died after coming home from a POW camp in Cambridge, and one other named Paul had been eight years in Russia. The father had also died in 1946 and they were finding it hard to make their farm pay.

27 August 1952 Wednesday

Had a nice breakfast though we didn't like the malt bread, then left about 7.30 on the road to Winterberg. We seem to meet some really nice people.

The journey to Winterberg was very tiring, uphill most of the way and unpleasant weather. Passed through several villages with huge piles of logs outside every house. The houses were covered in slates, and slate quarrying seemed to be the main industry. Reached Winterberg about 10.30 and were greeted with the sign NO. 6 LEAVE CENTRE. The town is way up in the hills and I suppose British troops could find healthy relaxation there. Passed straight on and set off down a hill towards Hallenburg, 15 Kms away. A small boy on a bike swerved in front of Irene and gave her a fright. The way to Hallenburg was all downhill and we carried on downwards right through the town. It was a lovely ride, couldn't believe the hill could keep on going so long. I bought some rolls and cakes in the village, then, just outside after we had climbed another hill, we lit a fire and made coffee. After that had a general sort out of kit, and wrote up the log.

Set out for Marburg 50 kilometres distance. We had not gone far when a lorry stopped for us and took us within 6 kms of the place. Cycled in and found the hostel. Ate some food, had a good wash, also washed some clothes. Then, feeling a lot more respectable we took a cycle ride around the town. Bought an aluminium pot for cooking, as we have found a large pot is necessary for our appetites. Later took a walk up a hill and looked down on the lights. Stew for super, cost 35 pfgs. Each.

28 August 1952 Thursday

Bought rolls and cheese for breakfast, had to get someone to wake Irene. Then set out towards Wurzeburg. Got as far as Kirchain and then decided to go through Alsfeld to Fulda as this seemed to be the best way. Travelled all day through very pleasant and easy country. Not much traffic and few hills. The weather was fine and sunny. Bought a midday meal in Alsfeld. Its an old-fashioned sort of town. All the local lads seemed to be fascinated by Irene's shorts. Towards evening we bought eggs and milk at a farm. The woman there also gave us a slice of bread, must have thought we were starving. They were most interested in us, and expressed wonder that we were going as far as Munich. I suppose it's the other side of beyond to them. Passed by the town of Fulda and camped in a wood full of sandpits, groped around for a long while, but couldn't find a level spot anywhere.

29 August 1952 Friday

Up at 6, made coffee and toast for breakfast. Also had a good wash out of a dixey. Left about 8. Headed for Wurzeburg. The countryside was extremely pretty. Not any of the rugged grandeur of mountains that make one dismal, but fine rolling hills with much grassland and pine forests. For we poor cyclists though, those hills were hardship. We would spend an hour walking up, and then down we'd come on the other side in five minutes. Then a mile or so on and the same thing again.

Palled up with a German lad from Bamberg. He was going our way. Invited us into a Gasthoff for dinner and bought us drinks. Also we shared his sausage which was good. The weather became extremely warm in the afternoon and we could sense the atmosphere of the south in the villages. A sort of easy-going sleepiness hung about them, and one could imagine oneself in Italy or Mexico. Made coffee by a brook and a little later the German said "goodbye" and hurried on.

It was about 6pm when we entered Karlstadt. There we bought food for our evening meal which we intended to cook before reaching Wurzeburg. We wanted to get some water and I got annoyed with my bike because it wouldn't stand up. Then a lorry driver came up and offered us a lift. I suppose we looked rather tired. Put our bikes on the lorry and sat in the back eating cold bacon sandwiches all the way to Wurzeburg. When we arrived we asked for the Anzback Road and were directed up another huge hill on the way to Frankfurt. It was nearly dark, we felt really tired. Spent a long time looking for a place to camp. Then met up with a German couple doing the same thing. We camped together on a hill overlooking the whole town. It was a terrific view. The German spoke English like an American and we sat up a while talking. I caught a head cold.

30 August 1952 Saturday

Stayed in bed till 8, admired the view over Wurzeburg, though we thought it noisy. Made coffee and fried bacon for breakfast. The other couple packed their kit and left. Then we had a bit of a wash and cycled back into the town. Irene cashed one of her traveller cheques. Left on the way to Munich. The cobbles were terrible until we reached open country. The weather was very hot and oppressive. Kept stopping for apples or pears by the roadside. A fellow caught us up, he could speak English and Esperanto, and seemed an exceptionally energetic sort of chap. He reckoned to do between 200 and 300 kms a day, and was on his way to Bologna and back in 16 days. He had come 90kms. From Frankfurt that morning. We were quite impressed. He was a nice chap.

Villages by the river that we were passing still seemed to have that sleepy southern atmosphere. Then at Ochsenfurt we turned up into the hills. I got a tow up with a farm tractor then went back and helped Irene. A little further on we decided we had done enough for one day in such hot weather, so we pushed our bikes up into a pinewood and cooked our meal. Remained in the wood until well after dark, then got ready to move by night. Thought it would be an experience worth trying. A wind blew up so suddenly that we thought a storm was coming, so took shelter beneath a bridge for an hour. The storm didn't come however, so we set off. It was cool and quite pleasant, but I felt tired. We would get off every time a car came and try to see the fruit trees by its headlight beam.

Stopped at a Gasthaus for water and learnt the time was 11.30. The place was full of activity. Later we stopped at another place and went in for a coffee. There were four men sitting at a table playing cards, and no other signs of life. We drank our coffee and went back into the night.

Eventually reached the town of Uffenheim. It seemed to be a very quaint old place by the light of the street lamps. We sat on a seat eating bread and sausage, though first we put a lot of warm clothes on. Left the town about 1.30 am and a few kilometres out felt so tired that we rolled a bed roll into a hollow and went sound asleep in spite of a few drops of rain.

31 August 1952 Sunday

Irene woke me up from a dead sleep to tell me a car was coming. We quickly sat up and watched it go by. They were surprised to see us. It must have been about 4 am. We cycled on as day was breaking, picked up a lot of pears and apples, but really felt too tired to be appreciative. Got to a lake and had a wash. I bought two eggs and we had breakfast. Loads of fried bread. Felt a bit better then and we went through Rothenburg. The impression one gets on first approaching is not very good, and really with the hundreds of Americans about, it looks nothing more than a tourist attraction.

We didn't stay long and set out down a hill on the way to Creglingen. Halfway down we saw a spot and decided to get some sleep. I pushed the bikes up a steep slope and over a potato field into a secluded spot, and we slept for three or four hours. Then I made some soup. It started to pour with rain just as we were packing up to go. Covered the bikes and kit with one gas cape, and ourselves crouched down low beneath the other. However the rain ran down our necks. Between lulls in the storm we ferried the bikes down. It was certainly a business getting them over the potato field. The mud clogged up the wheels and me, and I slipped and slithered all over the place. I took Irene's bike down by a different route, nearly dropped the thing, but it was better really. We were soaking wet, so went back to the hostel at Rothenburg and were thankful to change into dry clothes, and have a good meal. Spent the evening with a couple of German lads who spoke English. Walked around the town with them. Decided we were glad we had come back to Rothenburg as it seemed an interesting town in spite of all the American limousines. Wandered around the town a bit more, then about 6pm we met the same English lad that we had met at Dover and cycled to Brugge with. It was quite a coincidence. Walked down to the hostel with him and his friends.

Spent the evening talking to another English student who had hitch-hiked in with a coach tour. He gave us some delicious cream cakes. Previously that day we had stood outside a cake shop, mouths watering, perhaps Irene had been saying her prayers. It was a beautiful answer. Wrote a letter home. A party of English lads talked to us for a long while, thought we were Germans who spoke good English.

Rothenburg

02 September 1952 Tuesday

Irene wrote her letter and we prepared to go. The cook in the hostel who had been three years in America, asked us to fill in his visitors' book. Joined up with two German lads both going to Nordlingen. One of them spoke English. We had a really lovely day's ride. The country was pleasant and easy going, and we made each other good company. Shared our food at lunch time and made coffee. Sometimes we sang songs, English and German. Towards the end of the afternoon we lost the fellow who couldn't speak English and didn't see him again.

Rothenburg

Reached Nordlingen about 6, and went straight out again to buy food as there were self-cooking facilities in the hostel. My chain broke and cost 60pfgs. to be put right. Caused great amusement to Irene to see me peddling fast and nothing happening. I had a cold shower, then we ate a huge pile of fried potatoes, egg, sausage and bacon, though I couldn't find the latter. Later the warden took us for a walk around the town and showed us some beautiful old buildings, including the oldest shop in Germany. Then at ten o'clock we heard the traditional "so gesellen so" called from the clock tower, and answered by a policeman. The only thing about this performance was that the policeman didn't come out and answer until about 3 minutes after the fellow in the tower had closed his window and gone.

03 September 1952 Wednesday

Something wrong with the day somehow, perhaps we were a bit tired to start off with. Hans, our German pal whom we had come from Rothenburg with, decided to come with us. Took photos in Nordlingen then set out for Augsburg.; We did the 30 kms to Donauworth quite easily, except for a little tiff with Irene resulting in her cycling miles on her own. After Donauworth we bought food and had lunch. Nobody seemed to eat much, except me. Cycled on some more till about 4.30. The countryside looked much like Holland. Bought some cutlets and found a place to cook them. I cycled in to the next village for milk and water. Irene felt sick and missed her lunch which was a pity as Hans had cooked the cutlets divinely. Cycled the last 10 miles to Augsburg in the dark and found the hostel. It began to rain so we were glad we had not camped.

04 September 1952 Thursday

Irene still didn't feel good, no breakfast, it rained. Hans did his best to keep our spirits up as we were obviously going through a bad patch. Stayed in all morning, sat and played chess, while Irene slept. Went for a walk with Hans around the town after lunch. Irene came down for tea. Went out together for another walk. Ordered supper in a pleasant little gasthoff and a delicious meal was brought up. Then Irene felt sick again and couldn't eat, so Hans and I shared hers.

Hans our lifelong friend who we met in Rothenburg

05 September 1952 Friday

Irene woke up feeling fine and we set out for Munich. I felt quite sorry saying goodbye to Hans, he seemed so downhearted at parting. He insisted on paying the hostel fees, and we could do nothing to persuade him not to. "So that we would have enough to sleep in a hostel again tonight" he said.

We made good headway though it was a bit of a struggle to keep Irene going. Relations with her had become a bit strained. To me she seems to do a lot to hinder and nothing to assist. Still, perhaps I'm getting impatient. We met a student on the way riding a mini motor cycle. He seemed a bit of a crank, but showed us a map of Munich in order that we should find the hostel easily. Reached the town about .3.30. Seemed an awful long while getting through the outskirts. There was mail for both of us at the Telegrafi. Asked many people and at last reached the hostel. It is a big place and very free and easy. We went out shopping and bought some mutton to boil. Had a huge meal rounded off with flapjacks.

Spent the evening talking. The atmosphere more adventurous than anywhere previous. Germans round the piano sang really good rousing songs. Had a cold shower and did some washing, then went to bed, climbed six floors to get there.

06 September 1952 Saturday

Took things very easy in the morning and cooked a large real English breakfast. Stayed in the common room for an hour or so listening to a fellow play the piano. He really was good. Went by tram to the town centre and rushed to be at the town hall (rathaus) by 11. However we got there 10 minutes late for the performance of mechanical figures. It was raining pretty hard so we had a look around a couple of big shops. Noticed the great price reductions, and bought some ham. Felt very hungry and filled up with sweets. The weather showed no signs of improving so we set off for the museum. On the way we saw a fish and chip shop, and couldn't resist it. Had a good cheap plate of fish cakes and chips

The museum proved to be really excellent. We were kept most interested for nearly four hours. Started off by creeping around in dark little tunnels to see how mining was done. Then we went upstairs and worked a lot of mechanical models. There were also all sorts of musical instruments, cars, bicycles, and in fact nearly everything. Didn't have time to see a quarter of it. About 4 pm we met the two Australian girls from the hostel and we all went to the restaurant and had a bowl of soup and a glass of milk. We were quite perturbed when we found we had been charged twice what was on the menu for the milk. Seems we had been given double measure.

When the museum closed the Australians caught a tram to the hostel. Irene and I walked around and saw some low dives, ending with the famous 'Hoffbrauhaus'. It lived up to its reputation ok except that the class of people there seemed rather similar to The front at Southend-on-Sea on a Saturday night. We walked around in there for quite a while and then came away again seeing no point in spending a mark on a 'mass' of beer. Went back to the hostel and made supper, but I think we had had enough for one day, both our stomachs felt queezy.

Spent the evening studying maps and listening to the piano in the common room. Relations with Irene still seem a little wrong.

07 September 1952 Sunday

Got away from hostel about 10.30 having filled in an autograph for an Australian and overhauled the bikes. Went to the post to see if mail had arrived, met an Italian there from Catania in Sicily. He gave us his address and an invitation to call on him. Bought a sausage and roll then set out towards Rosenheim. The going was a bit hard at first. Saw some jet planes take off straight overhead, nearly burst our ear drums. The countryside became a lot more wooded. The houses had huge eaves and were highly decorated. In fact the whole place looked completely different to the part before Munich.

Reached Rosenheim about 3.30. Watched a highly decorated brewer's cart go through the streets. There seemed to be something happening though we could not discover what. It started to rain quite heavily now. It had been spitting a bit all day. Still we moved on towards Endorf and then Hem Hof where there is a hostel. It rained all the 18 kms. there, but we kept fairly dry thanks to the gas capes. Reached the hostel about 6 pm. Eating apples. Bought some soup for supper and they gave us hot water for coffee.

08 September 1952 Monday

It was a beautiful morning. Rose early and washed outside in a tree trunk hollowed out to make a water trough. Walked down the hill to the village and bought bread and cheese and jam for breakfast. All this was before 8 am., but things seem to get going early in Germany. Ate breakfast and slowly got kit assembled. We were in no hurry as we had only to go 30 km. to Traunstein. Left the hostel about 10. Met the old warden on the hill and shook hands goodbye. He wished us 'gute fahrte'. The warden and his wife were a nice old couple who had come from Konigsburg in Prussia, having been turned out by the Russians. They had had enough of wars.

The weather kept fine, though the air was light and fresh with some chill in it. We could see the mountains not far away to the west and south. With the Chiem See in the foreground they made a fine view. On either side of the road though, the countryside was flat and damp, much like Holland. Though it was well wooded which improved it a little. We saw some deer run off into a wood just outside Hem Hof. They had been lying in the sun.

Entered the little village of Seebruck. It is on the edge of the Chiem See in a beautiful spot. However it proved to be very much a holiday resort with many gasthauses, and signs about rooms vacant and car parks etc. We cycled through and out into the country again. I always feel a little more contented to be out of a built up district and in the countryside again. Sat by a road about 5 miles from Traunstein and ate our lunch. It was then we resumed our old relationship and the strained atmosphere of the past few days vanished.

Got into Traunstein about 12.15. I tried to decide which of the houses had been used as a troops' meal halt, but couldn't. Went to the post office for my trousers, but the poste restante was closed, so we made for the youth hostel. It was a small place with no cooking facilities. So after a quick meal we packed some things and went off into some woods and cooked a stew. The place we found was beside a stream, secluded and pleasant, until it started to rain. It was lucky we had everything finished. Back at the hostel we were given hot water for coffee. Spent the evening writing letters and studying the map. Decided to get to Italy as quick as possible.

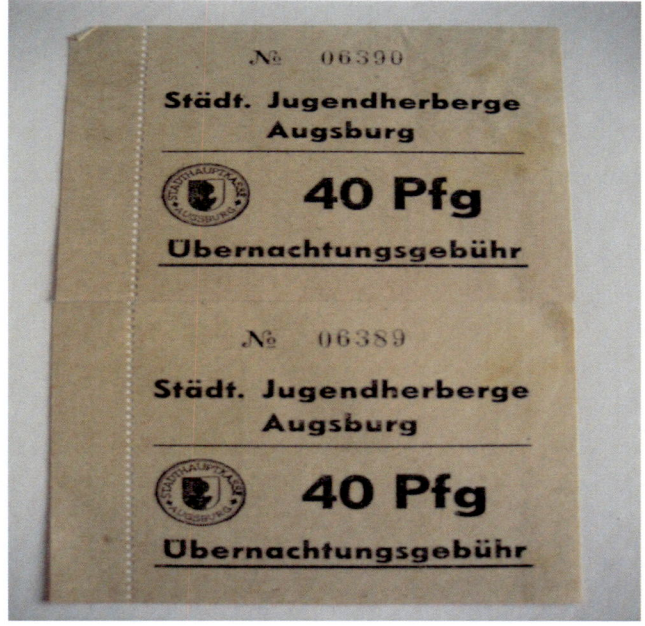

youth hostel tickets

09 September 1952 Tuesday

It was raining, we spent the whole morning waiting for it to stop. I went up to the post office and was glad to find my trousers had been sent on. It was cold so I put them on in a phone box. Bought some margarine, bread and sugar. We had been told it was rationed in Austria. The rain still hadn't stopped at 12.00 but we decided to make the best of it and get to Salzburg. I had spent a lot of the morning talking to a German student from Hanover, who studied in Marburg. He was quite content to remain for the day at the hostel.

The rain was not too bad when we set off, and after a while we had a long run downhill. It would have been lovely had the weather been good. The back wheel of my cycle went wrong and I had to turn the bike upside down to fix it. It was wet and windy at the time so I didn't like it.

AUSTRIA

The German side of the frontier was very easy, but it was a terrific palava to get into Austria. They wanted to see all my money, and then messed about with forms concerning the bikes. They ended up by clamping some sort of security tag on each of them. Within a few moments of crossing the frontier we were in Salzburg. Immediately noticed the large numbers of Americans about. First we made for the post and at the third attempt found the right post office. There was a letter for me only. The only news was that Colin was getting engaged! We found the hostel without difficulty, dumped our kit, and went straight out for a look at the town, also for some shopping. We bought cakes and ices and good meat before we realized that really things were no cheaper than in Germany. Still it was good while it lasted. Back at the hostel we lit a fire, made a meat pie and rice pudding which went down very very well. We talked with some Germans who had that day come over the Gross Glockner pass. They said there was a snow storm. That rather set us thinking, and we decided to ask at St Veib if the pass was open. Otherwise we would go to Badgastein and through the tunnel by train.

10 September 1952 Wednesday

We went again to the post in the morning, but there was nothing there. It rather shook me to have to pay 1.60 sch. to have mail forwarded to Lienz. We were struck by the large number of English people about. Went out on the road to Hallein. The weather was sunny and we took a photo of a castle of Salzburg.

In Hallein I got a spoke in my bike fixed, however the fellow who did it was not a good mechanic and took a lot of things to bits that weren't necessary, then put them back wrong. However I showed such surprise when he said the cost would be eight shillings, that he let me go for nothing. Still my bike didn't go properly, and we couldn't very well go back.

Gross Glockner

Had lunch in the sun by a rail crossing. We were really well into the mountains. We walked up a very steep hill and I had to have Irene's kit on my bike. At the top we talked to two ladies who advised us to go and look at a waterfall, however we pushed on. There was a river, railway and road, and the cliffs rose sheer on either side. We found the whole thing most oppressive. The grandeur was too much for us. Once the first impact of the mountain scenery is over the rest is easily foregetable. The thing we noticed as much as anything was the hard look about the people. They did not strike us as being particularly friendly. However we were given milk at a farm, also after two attempts, I managed to buy three eggs quite cheaply. We built a fire by the road and fried bread and fried eggs. We had lots of bread so felt quite full. It got dark and we were too far from the hostel at Zell am See so we looked out for a camp site. It was too dark to see much, and anyhow for a lot of the time we were between a very fast and sinister river, and the railway. Also the hills rose very steep on either side with not a chance of a tent site. I tried one likely spot, but there was a house near, and we did not fancy encountering the surly mountain folk at night. I turned the wheel of my bike round by the light of some factory. I had been forced to walk since we had our supper. Now it was on a very low-geared fixed wheel. At last we asked the keeper of a level crossing if there was a place, and he very kindly let us bed down in his hut. He moved his table, swept the floor and did a lot to make us comfortable. It was warm and we were very thankful to be there.

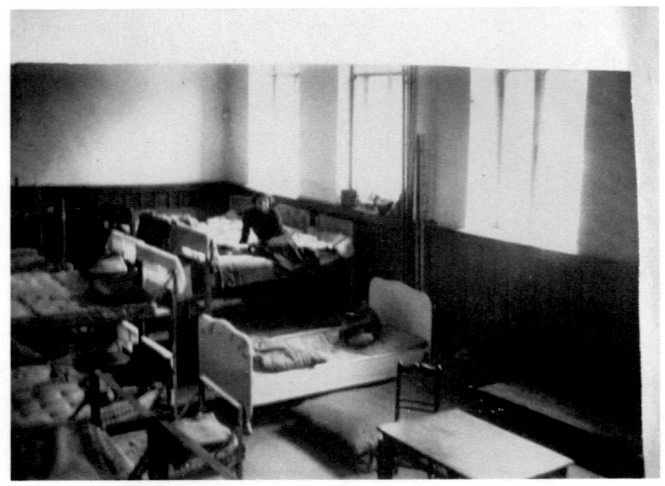

Irene in Zell Youth Hostel, the only woman there!

11 September 1952 Thursday

Left the crossing about 6.30. The morning was cold, but fine. We tried at several places to get eggs, but finally had to be contented with coffee, bread and jam. We made our fire on the parapet of a bridge, and caused great amusement to motorists passing. Still, it was near water and there was somewhere to sit. At the first attempt to boil water I kicked the pot over. We spent about two or more hours there getting washed etc., but we only had about 15 kms. To Zell so there was no hurry. We moved on again slowly, my bike was difficult to ride, and making all sorts of creaking noises. We watched them dissecting a cow in a field. They said it was full of grass, and the stomach when they brought it out swelled up terribly. It was quite a gruesome, though an interesting, sight.

I bought two eggs at a farm and four at another. Then later we got some milk so sat in a pleasant spot and fried more eggs and bread. Kept two of the eggs hard boiled for later. We had a good meal. Cycled into Bruch and spent about twenty minutes trying to hitch a lift over Gross Glockner, just on the off chance. However we thought really we would like to do it under our own steam, so left off for a day or so and went to Zell six Kms. further away.

Zell is a proper tourist spot, the shop keepers speak English, the prices are high, and as we have come to expect now, lots of Americans. The hostel caused great amusement as the warden there first asked us whether we would like a five or three schilling bed. Naturally we chose the three schilling. Then came a shock. She pointed to the top of two double-tiered bunks side by side. We were astounded and thought perhaps she had mistaken Irene for a boy. A German lad assured us it was quite usual in Austria, We couldn't help busting into fits of laughter. We wondered what they would think about it in England, but we settled down ok though. Had a quick wash then went out shopping. I changed an English pound for 62 Schilling. Had for supper a really good salad. There were no cooking facilities, but the woman gave us hot water. Spent most of the evening talking to an Austrian medical student. However he was rather a poor listener but quite interesting. Also he bought out his primus stove and some biscuits so we made coffee and tea. The German lad spoke good English but seemed to have got hold of the Goerdie way of saying "well" after every sentence. He did say "oh very nice" in a most amusing Oxford accent.

12 September 1952 Friday

It rained all day. Spent the morning arguing with a young German extremely pro-Nazi. The attitude seems to be that Germany is being treated unfairly. "Why can't we be given back our African colonies? Etc. They don't seem to realize that they caused the war and lost it. In the afternoon we played chess. I lost. Also went out shopping and bought a newspaper. Had a large meal of lettuce, sausage, cheese and tomatoes for supper. Spent the evening writing up my log and reading the newspaper. The weather was cold. Before bed I went for a short stroll through the town. It seemed dead.

13 September 1952 Saturday

Lay in bed till 8.15. I got up and got the breakfast. Used the last of the Nescafe. Went for a walk around the town and spent up two day's supply of money. We are on rather short rations owing to a few expenses. In the afternoon we went walking up the hill and looked at the aerial ropeway to the top of the hill. Walked through the woods overlooking the town, and down. Picked some apples on the way. Seem to spend a lot of time thinking about food. We are not hungry, but just fancy something civilized.

Watched a strange sort of game played with flat wooden plates that slid along the ground. The object seemed to be much the same as bowls. Went out scrumping wild apples and got some greengages as well. A lot of English and Americans came to the hostel, so we rather predominated. Didn't think much of two English students who were hitching. They swore quite a bit. Still it was interesting talking with them. It was a simply marvelous day. I have never seen the sun so bright. The mountains were covered in snow, but were clear and looked very near. We were given some jellied herrings for breakfast which filled us up very well. They came from three Germans who were travelling luxuriously in a van.

We didn't get away till one as we both had a good wash down, and got things organised a bit. Then we walked along the front into the sun and watched small boys fishing. They just threw in a line and pulled out a fish. It was so easy. Our main thoughts were still of food. We had completely spent our money ration. Not hungry though, just fanciful for a good HOT English meal with plenty of luxuries. Got back to the hostel and had the last of our food. Then we packed up some rice and soup cubes with the intention of going up to the woods and cooking it. However the sun went down and it looked cold so we borrowed a fellow's spirit stove and made soup.

Then we decided to blow a day's money and go to a gasthaus for supper. Boy what an evening! Two Americans and a Swede together with a big Englishman from Rugby. We all went up in the Swede's car. Had a real good meal. Then a band started playing. The locals started dancing and the American started buying drinks all round. We went upstairs and all did a bit of dancing. Had fun with a local named Willie who had been two years in America. Got back feeling quite merry. The evening a huge success.

15 September 1952 Monday

CROSSING GROSS GLOCKNER

We didn't move off early as planned. I think the evening activities were rather to blame. I went out and got some shopping and we eventually left the hostel about 10. The weather was not pleasant, half rain and half not, just damp. Still we went pretty easily and soon arrived at Bruch. From there the road rose bit by bit until about 3 and a half miles from Bruch we had to get off and walk. The countryside was quite magnificent. It rose fairly sharply on either side of us until it disappeared in a cloud. Occasionally there was a waterfall. However we have seen so much mountain scenery that it ceases to impress us greatly. Shortly after getting off and walking Irene and I had a slight disagreement which caused me to sling my bike on the ground in disgust. (to our mutual regret later). The disagreement was not much really. I have a tendency to be impatient and when anything is wrong Irene does nothing more than moan about it. Still we got things straightened out then and they kept that way thereafter, which was a good thing as we had a lot to put up with.

After walking upwards for three or four kilos we reached Ferleiten and bought, for five schillings, two tickets to go over the road. The woman selling them to us was a miserable young character. I also managed to buy a loaf of white bread in a gasthof. The road became quite steep and we pushed steadily upwards resting at every kilometre for a short while. I had a rope from my bike to Irene's and gave her some help to get up. This amused bus loads of tourists that kept passing. It made me sweat a bit.

By the time we had done five kilos from Ferleiten and reached the 700 u.d.m. mark we had had enough, and decided to try and make some tea. We were in a cloud, and everything was soaking wet, but after several attempts, and shaving the bark off lots of twigs, we managed to get a fire going. Then we drank the most delicious cup of tea, and had some of our sandwiches. After that we spent some time collecting wood and made a huge fire which warmed us and the whole area. We were camped right on the bend of curve 7 and our fire must have looked quite strange to motorists coming down the hill. We got several waves from people snugly tucked up in cars and buses, but we didn't envy them, and rather looked forward to camping at over 5000 feet. We built another big fire to dry the grass where our tent would be pitched. Before that two German cyclists walking up stopped and told us that we had eight kilos before going down a bit, and that we would then have to go up again. We quite rejoiced at the thought of only '8 kilos more' and then it dawned on us that it was five miles - upwards. The Germans were staying at a hostel in Hoch Mais, a kilometre further, but the fee of 8 schillings was too much for us. We got the bedding etc., down and then put huge rocks around the fire in the hope that it would stay alight till morning. As a precaution we littered the area around the tent with pots, bits of wood and string, in the hope that any intruder would make a noise and warn us. The tent was warm and comfortable - at first.

16 September 1952 Tuesday

The sun shining on distant mountains.

Gross Glockner

We both slept lightly, but managed to keep fairly warm and comfortable; I got up first shortly after it was light. The view simply took my breath away. The cloud was just below us and above the sun was shining on the mountains. They were covered in snow and with the blue sky behind made the most beautiful view I have ever seen. They came as quite a shock as well because we had arrived in dense cloud and had no idea they were there at all. We took two photographs. The fire was still hot and we soon had it blazing away. The cloud kept lifting and enveloping us then dropping again showing the mountains. There wasn't much for breakfast and the tea got stewed a bit through being left too near the fire. Still we filled up with bread and milk. .

Three Germans, two men and a woman, travelling in a Volkswagen, stopped by and took some photos. Just as they were leaving they took some of us and I of them, and they promised to send us a copy back to England. I don't think the woman trusted us much. She gave us a chocolate and seemed in a hurry to go, but the men were quite nice, though of the 'steady-job-and security' type.

We started up the hill as before but with a bedding roll on the handlebars to make pushing easier. It was real heavy going and although we rested every kilometre we got very tired. The views were magnificent. We got beyond the clouds and past the tree line, and began to see patches of snow about. We had a long rest and ate sandwiches after four kilos, and then pushed on for three more kilos to the first high point. That last three kilos was gruelling. We could see the road up above us, and it looked so far and high. Still at last we got to the collection of buildings and restaurants at the height of nearly 8,000 feet.

Some Americans asked to take photos of us, so we let them. We managed to cut off about a kilo of the road by climbing down an embankment. Then we had a glorious 10 minutes run downhill. Had to let air from the tyres as decrease in pressure made them too hard. We hadn't noticed them becoming hard while walking uphill and it wasn't until riding on the way down that we noticed the difference. We were now on the weather side of the mountain. It was a lot colder and began to get cloudy. Also the wind blew, which I think was worst of all. We pushed on though, kilo at a time, and got up to the first tunnel. It wasn't too long, but the wind simply whistled through. At the other side we had another slight run down. Then we clambered down into an old water course and ate the rest of our food. After the food we started going up again. It was freezing cold, and we could not see for cloud. We got to the next tunnel feeling just about all in. At the other side we were overjoyed to find that we had reached the highest point. 'Hochtor' 2500 metres U.D.M. We certainly felt relieved to think no more hill climbing, just plain sailing down. There was a house there and we got some hot water and made some Oxo. Then we wrapped up very warm and started going down. It was still hard to see, and the brakes were wet and didn't work so well, so we changed over bikes for a while. Felt sorry for cyclists we saw still on the way up. We soon got down among the trees again, and then felt rather cheated as we had to walk upwards for about another mile. Then it was easy going right into Heiligenblut which we reached about 3.30.

A small boy showed us the hostel. A jovial looking old woman told us to make ourselves comfortable in the kitchen. It was warn there. We got all our kit in as well. I went shopping and changed another English pound. The kitchen was very simple and not too clean, but we were allowed to cook on the stove and made a huge meal. The people interested us. There was the old woman, her husband, I think, and a small boy. They lived a very simple life and the supper they ate didn't seem to be much. It began and finished with many mumbled and not sincerely said prayers. The woman would mumble something, then the man would cut in and so on. There was just one pot in the middle of the table and each took turns to dip into it. Irene washed out some clothes, I hung up the tent to dry. Then about 8.30 we were shown a room with a huge pile of blankets and 8 camp beds. We made ourselves comfortable with a dozen blankets each and slept like logs.

Irene

With our bikes

17 September 1952 Wednesday

Got away from the hostel early as it was a school and the children started that day. Watched them all lining up to scrape their boots before going in. Cycled down and down through the valley until we reached Winklern. Then there was another long walk up. We picked a lot of apples to keep us going. At the top of the hill we crossed the county line and the road immediately deteriorated. A little way down was a beautiful view into a valley and we stopped and ate our jam sandwiches. Later on the view was even more magnificent. We were high up and could see for miles either side. The town of Lienz to the right and the road we would have to take stretching out eastwards. Went down the hill at a terrific speed and cycled into Lienz. The atmosphere looked definitely Italian, though there seemed to be a lot of blonde-haired people about. It was quite hot. There was no mail at the post office.

And so our Gross Glockner adventure had ended and we headed for Lienz

Left Lienz on the road for Obdrausburg, but a short way out we stopped by a stream for a good wash. Irene wrote a letter. The stream was cold but it was lovely washing in the sun. Got to Oberdrauburg about 5.30 and did some shopping. Then we turned south on the road to Udine and up another hill.

The road went back and forth up the side of a valley and we thought we'd never reach the top. I went to a café for water and got charged a schilling. The woman said there was none on the 'borg' yet a little further on we found a spring. Got to the top as it began to get dark. Built a huge fire and made a terrific mutton stew. It really filled us.

Slept in a wooden hut by the road, used for storing grit. Very comfortable. Sometime during the night we were awakened by a man carrying a lantern and leading a cow going past us. We lay very still and he passed without seeing us.

18 September 1952 Thursday

Got up at first light and had toast and jam for breakfast. Then we went down the road a few kilos and found a delightful spot to wash in. It was a stream by the road with grass growing either side for 100 yards or so, and then pinewoods rising until they ended in the mountains. The sun was shining and we had a pleasant wash. Then I sat on a stone and wrote my letter. Had another long run downhill to the village of Katsach. Spent the rest of our Austrian money on some sausage. Then started another long climb up towards Monte Crose and the pass into Italy. We were lucky to get a lIft on a lorry for four kilos. It was a big help uphill. The road was only a dirt track and seemed very unused, though a couple of cars (one English) had passed us. The valley rose almost sheer on either side. There was a great deal of timbering in progress. We passed a war cemetery. Don't know whether it was Austrian or German.

Eventually we got to some sort of Gasthaus. It was a gruelling climb. We seemed to be in a flat space between the hills, but after a kilo or so we started going up again. So we sat down first and ate half a loaf of bread and our sausage. Then did the last lap up to the frontier.

ITALY

It was no trouble getting through the customs. We noticed the difference in the appearance between the Italian officials and the Austrian. About 100 yards over the frontier the road turned left. In front it looked as though there was a sheer drop for a thousand feet into the valley. When we looked over the edge the sight really startled us for we could see about 20 or more layers of the road, each layer at a different level, the bottom one perhaps not more than 50 or 60 yards further out than the one at the top. It seemed a masterpiece of road making though it was still only a rough track, and the thought of cycling down rather peeved Irene. Still, after changing bikes and several rests we got to the bottom. It was freezing cold, the cloud was low, there was every evidence of landslides, and the atmosphere of the place rather disheartened us. We passed the village of Timou. It looked really poverty-stricken, nothing but hovels as dwellings. Irene was impressed by the utter change in everything. The people looked and acted differently. The houses and fields were different, and I think for the first time we realised just how far we were from England. The road was still very bad with lots of loose stones, and we were still going downhill. Just outside Paluzzi Irene fell off, and I fell off. The road was so bad. Irene hurt her leg and felt shaken. I was impressed by the way people came quickly to help. A man picked the bikes up, and got us water. Realized how lost I was as regards language. I just couldn't say a word. After a bit of a rest we went on some more and had a cup of coffee in a bar. It cost 30 lire, which was quite cheap. The weather was still miserable and had an ominous look. Irene's one wish was to get away from the mountains. We bought food in Tolmezzo, and then by an army camp we made a fire and cooked supper.

When it was dark, and after much groping around, we got the tent up. A sentry kept flashing a searchlight suspiciously, but we were left in peace.

19 September 1952 Friday

We had no bread for breakfast, but made do with a kilo of potatoes and two hard-boiled eggs. The sergeant from the army camp came over and told us we must leave as it was a prohibited area. We didn't hurry, and soon he was back again and stayed till we left.

It hadn't been possible to get a wash and we didn't feel too good. Actually I think our appearance is deteriorating daily. My hair is hanging around my ears, and we have used all the boot polish. We stopped by a bridge over a river and spent about two hours washing all the pots and pans and ourselves. Then it rained hard so we hung around under bridge for another hour. We moved on wearing gas capes and the weather gradually got better.

At Tricesimo we were just about starving. The bread shop was closed for siesta, so we went into an osteria and had two plates of spaghetti each. Irene caused some amusement at her attempts to eat the stuff, and two people tried to show her. However, it was jolly good and we felt better for it. Then we bought two apples and cycled to Udine. I asked for the poste and was given direction in German. We are generally taken for Germans here. There were two letters each for us. One of mine had been forwarded from Halingen in Holland to Munster and Munich in Germany and then to Salzburg in Austria. Then it turned out to be one of Mum's quick notes. Bought rolls and headed for

VENICE

There was a huge bank of thunder clouds behind us which looked most threatening and made us hurry. We got to Palmonova and into shelter just before the storm broke. We were mighty thankful, it was a terrific affair. After we had been sheltering for half an hour and eaten some sugared rolls, a tall Italian who had been talking in a butcher's shop, came up and spoke to us. When he learnt we had cycled from England there were many 'bravos' all round. He took us to a bar and bought coffee and cake for Irene. Then we went back to our bikes and spoke with the butcher in German. They gave us the impression that they would fix us up for the night. However the tall Italian said goodbye, and gesticulated towards the butcher's shop saying something about 'louis'. So we waited till Louis closed. That was at about 8. He came and asked us if we had anywhere to go, which seemed a silly question. However he got a fellow to take us to a farmyard in the town saying 'maybe' we would be alright. We were lucky and were allowed to sleep in a warm hayloft.

20 September 1952 Saturday

Got away from the farm at 6.30 and had a look around Palmonova. Italian troops were in the barracks where I was stationed. I was glad to get another look at them. We bought some eggs and were given some very rough salt by a baker who spoke English. Then we set off towards Sevignano. We made one attempt at finding firewood, but it proved impossible. There were flat cultivated fields on either side and the only wood I could find was from a soft prickly type of tree. It wasn't much good. A little later though we found a spot with enough to make a pot hot. We put four eggs in and had a good breakfast. On the whole things seem to be a lot dearer in Italy, except for simple country products. Butter for instance is 10/- a pound, so I suppose margarine will correspond. It rather looks as though we shall be living on vegetables, fruit, bread and eggs.

Had a general clean up after breakfast, and I changed the tyres on Irene's bike as the back one kept going flat. However it did no good and I was resolved to periodic pumping. Then, I don't know why, perhaps I was tired and worried, but Irene's can on the back of her bike kept rattling, and I tried fixing it, but couldn't. Somehow I lost my temper and threw it in the ditch. It was horrible for a moment till I calmed down, then I felt better. It is at times like this that Irene's great stoicism is a blessing.

At San Giorgo we bought some food and just outside had an excellent salad. Potatoes, tomatoes, cheese and onion all chopped up and sprinkled with sugar. It did a lot of good. After we had packed up and started again, a van stopped and the driver offered us a lift. It was wonderful. He took us 70 kilos to Treviso and bought us a coffee at Portogruaro. At Treviso we made a dash for the bank but it was closed.

St Mark's Square - Venice

Our appearance, especially Irene's shorts, seem to draw much attention. We walked around and spent our last 50 lire on bread. The tyre was again troublesome and I had to keep pumping it. We went towards Venice. It was a long main road with trolley bus lines, so after filling our water bottles at a village 'fontano' we turned right, then left, and on an impulse I cycled into a farmyard and asked to pitch our tent. They said we could and offered the use of their kitchen, so we were well set for the night. We made our meal in a large room, the only furniture being a table, sideboard, stove (very shiny), and some chairs. They gave us some of their food and wine. Everything seemed very simple, but interested us a lot. I offered a cup of tea, it was passed around with much interest. Plenty of straw in the tent, and we slept.

21 September 1952 Sunday

We slept warm and comfortable with so much straw in the tent. Got up about 6.30. All the family were well astir. The old Mama was away at church. We made tea, and had rolls and sugar for breakfast. It dawned on me that it was Sunday and we had no money. Hoped to be able to change a cheque at a station.

Irene was advised not to wear her shorts, as the old lady might object. She came in as we were having breakfast, and seemed in a very bad temper. For breakfast she poured coffee and milk over bread and a very little sugar, and sat well away from the table and ate it. The rest of the family started preparing for church, except one of the boys. It was quite a transformation. The old woman put her dirty clothes on, and immediately looked an old hag. She's not so old really.

We packed our kit, took a photo of the only boy left, and said goodbye. After pumping Irene's tyre twice in the course of a mile, I decided to have another go at finding the puncture, and this time was lucky enough to do so. It was in a spot already patched twice, so to make a good job of this patch we decided to leave it for half an our or so to set. In which time we wrote our logs. There were lots of people passing, and one old tramp asked us for money. Again we seem to cause a lot of attraction. I don't believe people in Italy quite understand us, and they are a little narrow minded in their outlook.

We put things together again and soon cycled through Mestre and along the five mile causeway to Venice. Irene was struck by the number of people about in Mestre. They seemed to be mostly men, all dressed up in their Sunday best. Italians look quite dandified and spivish with their drainpipe trousers, and dainty shoes.

My first impression of Venice was akin to that one gets along the Southend front. Still perhaps that's because we saw first the part near the station. I managed to cash a £5 traveller's cheque, and then we felt safe in eating our one and only roll left. We were ravenous. Parked the bikes, and got a water bus to the Casa San Giorno. The people at the start knew all about it, and put us on the right boat. But we were carried two stops past our destination. However we were taken back for nothing, and soon found the place. It was just like a youth hostel, though without cooking facilities. We were allowed to wash and change, but had to leave again until it opened at 6 pm.

Our main interest was food, and we set out with the object of buying some rolls and cheese. However it was siesta time and the only shops open were greengrocers, patisseries and cafes. After some fruitless searching, and spending odds and ends of money on tit bits, we got to the Piazza San Marco. For atmosphere it was wonderful. There were three bands playing in various cafes around the square. The whole place was packed with people (nearly all tourists) and there were lots and lots of pigeons. Really it was hard to describe things as they happen Venice. We wandered down many alleys, past numerous shops (always staring longingly at the cake displays), and eventually bought two dishes each of some filling pasta at a place called 'Pardonone'. Then again, feeling much more satisfied more alleys, more shops, and the Piazza San Marco. We bought a delicious substance in a bottle called Yogort. Back to the hostel. The shops were open again, and we bought rolls, jam and cheese, and had a supper.

Went out about 8am and bought lots and lots of rolls. Together with cheese, jam and sausage, we made a good breakfast. Then cut up the rest of the rolls for lunch time. We were determined not to be as hungry as we were yesterday. Spent the morning in St. Marco. Don't like the way it has been adapted for tourists. The view from the balcony into the square was excellent though. Wandered down the Via Garibaldi and looked at the shops there. It was a cheap centre.

Caught a boat to the lido and intended to be on the beach all afternoon. We were disgusted to find that entry to the beach was 280 lire each. So we sat on a seat for dinner. Had a look over the casino. It was a gorgeous place, but lifeless. Then we both went to sleep in the sun for another short while. Caught a boat back to St Mark's and sat for an hour in the square drinking coffee. The bill rather spoilt the effect though. It was enormous.

Went to the post office for mail, then over the Ponte Rialto and looked through another cheap bazaar. Met two Australians staying at the hostel . They were in the Ristorante Sociale where you get a meal for 150 lire. Walked back with them past the red light area to the hostel. Spent the rest of the evening talking with the Australians, a Pole and a Canadian. Think we like the country best and shall be glad to leave Venice tomorrow. Money worry is rather getting on our nerves (mine especially).

23 September 1952 Tuesday

NAPLES

From Venice, at our present spending rate, we would have enough money to get us across northern Italy and up to Paris through France. Then Irene said "I'd love to see Naples." Bless her!"

There was no way we could cycle south to Naples and not run out of money, so we decided to hitch-hike. Walked a long way through Venice alleys to the Rialto Bridge, and called at the post office. No mail, it was about 11 am. Caught a boat down the Grand Canal to the station. There was quite an argument with the cycle attendants but after some time we got away with paying only 100 lire instead of two. It was a really hot day. Spoke for a few moments with a Swiss lad. He was hitching to Genoa and then hoped to work a passage to Africa.

At the entrance to the Padua Autostrada we stopped a good while trying to get a lift. Then Irene's tyre went flat and I had to take it to bits, as usual couldn't find the puncture. Felt horribly nervy as we were going along I think it was the puncture and worry about all the money we had spent. Stopped at a cheap looking osteria and paid 800 lire for a lunch. I think we needed it and it did us good. Cycled on a bit, but again Irene's bike was giving trouble. Stopped at a repairers and got the lot done, including a new inner tube, for 400 lire. Felt better after that and we soon reached Padua. Bought some biscuits to ease the appetite and then a little way out of town we made a fire and had bread and milk. Tried again for a lift, but it was dark, so no luck. Anyhow we had a couple of cycles to pace us and it developed into quite a race for about 20 kilos. We enjoyed it fine. Asked at a house for a place to camp, a young girl there spoke English. We were shown a good grassy spot. Slept warm and well.

Friendly people we met near Naples on the road to Rome

24 September 1952 Wednesday

Woke up early and discovered that we were sleeping right next to a grape vine so made a start with a bunch each. Some little children watched us eat breakfast, wash and pack. Then the old man from the house vainly shooed them off. First I took photos of them and their address. They kept bringing us grapes and apples. Nice children.

We made good headway and soon crossed the River PO into Ferrara. Didn't stay there long, but set out on the road to Ravenna. Cooked a dinner of rice and oxo with an egg mixed in it. Then after we had messed about doing odd jobs for a while, we set off again. However, Irene said she felt tired and couldn't go faster etc. and for 20 Kms. We dragged along at a sole-destroying pace. The only consolation was the delicious apples growing everywhere. After Alphonine Irene quickened a bit and we went fine for about 6 kms. Then a small three wheeled motor cycle carrier stopped and we got a lift for nearly 100 miles through Ravenna, Rimini and Pesara to Ancona. We were dropped off there at 10 pm. Feeling tired and hungry. First we went to a restorante and bought spaghetti. Then bedded down in a ploughed field. It was a beautiful night, we slept immediately.

25 September 1952 Thursday

Got up at daybreak, but hadn't had too long sleep so felt tired. Cycled a couple of kilos to Ancona and bought milk and bread for breakfast. Made a good meal sitting on a wall by the road. Irene didn't like the cheese I bought, which rather annoyed me. We sort of by passed Ancona and walked up a long hill on the road to Pescara. On the other side we sat on a wall to write our letters. At the same time we thumbed lorries in the hope of a lift as we felt too tired to cycle. After about an hour a truck stopped and took us 25 kms. To Porte Ricinonte. Then we sat on a bridge for three hours and finished the letters. I went into the town and bought some spaghetti and was told how to make it. We moved up the road a bit and cooked our meal in a pleasant spot with lots of wood about. There was a group of Dutch people there all travelling in a small bus.

The spaghetti was ok, but I don't think I made it wet enough. It was about 4 o'clock by the time we had finished dinner and we decided a lift was just about hopeless, and to cycle on again. Went about 30 kilos and then stopped by a tap for a wash as we had been all day without one. I had just got myself stripped and ready when a huge lorry stopped and the driver started washing down his number plates. I asked if they were going our way, and after some persuasion got them to take us the 300 kms to Foggia.

The cab of the truck was huge and comfortable. There were two beds behind the seat. Irene spent the whole journey sleeping on one. The two drivers took it in turns doing 4 hours each. The one not driving slept in the other bunk. In this manner they kept the lorry going for the whole journey and only stopped once at midnight for a meal. There was a puncture and it took about 10 minutes to change the wheel. I slept quite a bit by lying along the seat. We arrived at a petrol station in Foggia about 4.15 am. A distance of 200 miles in 10 hours. A pretty good average for a heavy truck.

26 September 1952 Friday

We were both mighty tired and dirty at the tankstelle but the people there were very nice. Showed us a place to wash and promised to get us a truck to Naples. First though we had two delicious cups of creamy coffee. Irene didn't feel so good so we were allowed to sit in a lounge. Shortly after daybreak a fellow asked us in broken English if we would like to go in his truck to Naples. We were highly pleased at this and got our kit over by the truck ready. Then when the other driver came he said 'no' we couldn't come. Still with such a start we weren't much perturbed or disappointed. The staff at the station changed over at 8 am and the new staff mended the puncture in Irene's bike and also fitted a complete new piece into the old tyre that I had patched so many times.

At nine Irene went to the bank and cashed a travellers' cheque. Then we went across the road to a Trattoria and had a not so good meal for 600 lire. However, there is so much taste and flavouring to this Italian food that I felt quite satisfied. Went to sleep in the lounge at the station, and Irene got talking with a clerk there. We have met with a lot of narrow-mindedness amongst Catholic races, so we find it best to describe ourselves as brother and sister. The young book-keeper was trying hard to make a good impression when I awoke.

About 1 we got a truck going to Naples. Piled the bikes on top of a load of melons and off we went. There was a jolly crowd of five in the wagon and we two made seven. By sitting on the bed at the back we were all quite comfortable, though it was rather warm. We soon got up among the hills. The general colour of the land is brown. There are few trees and every sign of soil erosion. The people appear to live in hovels, and do not look at all friendly.

While back at the Tankestelle we had mentioned that perhaps we should cycle to Naples, and the people there wouldn't hear of it. 'Banditti' they kept saying. Now we began to understand why. I don't think it would have been a good spot to camp. The towns are generally built on a high altitude. Everyone in them seems to bring his occupation into the street. The whole atmosphere is far more Arabic than European. Before dark we stopped at a café for food. It was an interesting and surprising experience. All we could see on entering were three tables covered with scraps of food, and simply crawling with flies. A youngish woman was eating.

Within a moment one of the crew had helped himself to a piece of pastry-like stuff she was eating, and passed it around to us. It was hot but practically tasteless. The crew quickly got themselves bread and started eating huge sandwiches containing pickled egg plant. We were given about half a loaf with some in. It tasted very pleasant. Still, we felt hungry. It seemed a very queer system altogether. The five men just walked around in and out of the café helping themselves to what they could. They poured me out a tumbler of very rich port-like wine. After about 20 minutes a table was cleared of it's oddment, (they went on the floor). Serviettes and tumblers were put out and we all sat round eating bread. Also a piece of sausage. I noticed one of the men dipping his bread in wine. Then up came huge plates of spaghetti. They really were huge. Irene couldn't get through hers though I enjoyed mine. The men made a horrible noise eating it.

After the spaghetti came meat that had been grilled. It was tender, though a bit smokey. With the meat we ate lettuce and pickled egg plant. Of course the wine was flowing all the time, and I think they got through about 6 litres altogether. It was gratifying, however, to note that one of the drivers did not drink alcohol. The whole meal was most satisfying, though really it wasn't treated as a meal (not by English standards). Everyone did just as they liked and behaved as they liked. A couple of the men were quite merry and spent a long time trying to make me drink more wine. Eventually I did drain if off quickly and discovered, for a joke, they had put salt in it. We didn't have to pay for the meal though I asked about it. We drove on for another half hour. Everyone was singing though the type of singing seemed much akin to Arabic. Also one of them who had drunk quite a lot kept talking to us and shaking hands. Actually it was, I think, just an excuse to touch Irene. He did this in a most embarrassing way, and Irene had to be most firm.

We stopped at another café and were bought an excellent cup of café latte. Then away again, talking and singing all the way through Benevento until we came to Afragola, a town about 5 miles from Naples. The men immediately set about unloading the melons, told us we could sleep in the cab and not to worry about the bikes. We slept soundly and awoke to find ourselves in the middle of the town market square with dozens of curious children peering in at us. Those five men had treated us wonderfully "Attentione a Napoli" one of them said as we thanked them and said goodbye.

Naples is the most squalid, dirty, stinking town I have ever come across. Far worse than anything I'd seen when serving as a soldier in Egypt. We got to the hostel at 8.45. Had time for a quick wash and then left with a bundle of washing. Couldn't find a laundry anywhere.

Bought some rolls and ate soup in a sort of grocery snack bar. It filled us up fine. But I can still remember the bits of pig skin with bristles still showing. We must have been terribly hungry. Walked around and got stung 90 lire each for white coffee. We made the mistake of sitting down to drink it. Walked around a bit, saw a nun begging in the street, and looked in shacks with just enough room for a bed and nothing else. Went to a theatre at midday. The chap on the door expected a tip. Most disappointed in us. The show seemed to consist of three very amateurish female singers and a rather colourless funny man, and a fellow who could sing Italian songs really well. You can notice a sort of half and half between ordinary and Arab music.

After the theatre my stomach started rebelling at the soup from the morning. That was when I began to dislike Naples. Bought a Readers' Digest and Telegraph and sat in the station buffet for two hours reading. Hostel at eight, bread and jam supper on the roof. The only place where the air was cool. It still stank though. Washed the sheets.

28 September 1952 Sunday

Sat on the roof for a couple of hours while the clothes dried. Felt horrible and had to keep running. The very thought of that soup made me feel sick. Left about twelve. The sun was boiling. Made good progress on the road to Rome.

HEADING FOR HOME

After 30 kms. it was getting towards evening. I went to a house for water and a couple of eggs Got them, then the old woman asked us to sit down, and gave us some grapes. The next door neighbours came in. One man spoke English and his brother German. The one who spoke German took us next door to his house, gave me wine and let us cook our supper on his gas. He cooked the eggs for us. After I took a photo of the whole family. Very pleasant meal. Slept in a field a few kilos from Capua. It was a beautiful night. Warm moonshine and starry.

29 September 1952 Monday

Up at dawn, moved off the field and sat by a track for breakfast. All we had was bread and milkless tea. Dipped the bread in tea, then in sugar. Ate lots of it and felt fairly satisfied. Cycled towards Farmua. Italian men cyclists seem to like tailing us. On many occasions we have as many as three or four hanging on behind. We refer to them as our shadows. There were three on the way to Farmua.

Stopped and picked some grapes, got my shirt ripped on the barbed wire. Even here we can see a steady improvement in the people. The towns and villages don't stink so much. Went up hill for a good long way. Grapes everywhere. Then down for a lovely long stretch to Farmua. Arrived about 2.10. Did some shopping in the market there. An old fellow spoke English, turned out to be an Italian American. He was very proud of an invite he'd had to an 'at home' with the US Ambassador.

A few miles out of Farmua we stopped and cooked ourselves a 'one-pot'. Just at the end we were feeling like a sweet and along came a fellow who gave us four lovely bunches of grapes. They were a real round off for the meal. Then it started raining and we took shelter by a lime pit. Sat in front of a lorry there for nearly two hours and talked a lot with the driver. The same person who gave us the grapes. There were women working there and we were told their wage was 30 lire an hour (about 5p). It was horrible work all among the lime, yet they do it for 10 hours a day.

After the rain we went up hill for along while. Near the top stopped at a Casa Cantoneira for a wash. The woman thought Irene mad to wash her feet in cold water. There was a terrific run down the other side of the hill for about 5 miles to the town of Fondi. Bought a few things for supper The weather looked very threatening so a short way out we asked at another Cantoneira to sleep in a garage for the night. They were quite agreeable. Swept it out for us and laid down cardboard. Ate our supper by candlelight.

30 September 1952 Tuesday

It rained all morning and we were stuck in the garage with lots of flies for company. The woman asked Irene if she would like to use the lavatory, also bought us some apples which I think was very good of her. The rain hung off for a bit at midday and we set off. Irene, as usual, was starving, we speculated on the chances of her having worms! Anyhow bought half a loaf, split it down the middle, put sliced sausage between, and ate a good meal going along. Then I pinched a few grapes for afters.

At one point we cycled 25 miles along a dead straight road. We went very fast and I think made up for a lot of lost time. At Cistern we bought some bread and jam, then cycled out looking for a place to make tea. Irene said she would like to look around a cemetery we were passing. While she was looking I got talking to the lodge keeper, with the result that we were invited to make our tea at his fire place. He quickly lit the fire and set a table and chair for us. That was all very fine the weather was miserable out. He told us a lot about the British soldiers being there during the war and also about the fighting. Cistern is not far from Anzio.

We left towards dusk having refused his offer for us to sleep there. We wanted to get ahead some more. A few miles further on going downhill, Irene caught her wheel in a level crossing and fell off. She was rather shaken and had grazed her legs. I asked at an office if she could rest there a little. The people were very kind. Bathed her grazes and gave her a glass of milk, me a glass of some kind of liquour. They thought it rather queer of Irene not to drink. The office turned out to be part of a house, and we were invited to sleep in the office all night. This was wonderful as I was a bit dubious of our chances of finding anywhere that late, and the weather was still too bad for camping. The family were about middle class, and we noticed a great difference in their way of life. It was far more like the English, and they seemed to find a lot to laugh about. In the usual Italian fashion they went to a lot of trouble to make us comfortable, and even brought a little bed for Irene. Gave us some excellent grapes. We lay in the dark office and could just hear some modern music from their wireless. It was the first we had heard for ages, sounded wonderful. Went to sleep happy

01 October 1952 Wednesday

Got up about 6.30. The people made hot water for us and we had breakfast at a table outside. It was very pleasant and finished up with more grapes. Took a photo before leaving, then cycled 40 kms. Into Rome. The last part of the journey was quite hectic. The Italian drivers have no road manners at all, and to them a cyclist doesn't count. Coming down a long hill into the city was a nightmare. The traffic coming up just came straight out to overtake and forced us to swerve and brake a lot. Neither did the people particularly impress us when we got to the city. They seemed rude and ill mannered. It took about an hour to see if we had mail at the post office and arrange to have it forwarded to Pisa. They went through a lot of form filling and even wanted to know where my passport was issued.

Bought some food and sat for an hour on a seat to eat it. Then going down a hill of wet cobbles Irene fell off again. She was not really hurt but her nerves were very shattered. Immediately a crowd gathered, some well meaning and others there just to stare. A man and woman kept insisting she go to a doctor or pharmacy, though it would only have been a waste of money. They didn't realise that all she wanted was to rest and be quiet. Still it started to rain again and that soon cleared them off. A cup of café latte in a bar put her right again. Then we went around a couple of tourist visiting spots and didn't know what they were.

We crossed the River Tiber, bought a real good ice in the Piazza St. Peter, then visited the church of St Peter. That really is wonderful and extremely impressive. After the church we went rash and bought another ice cream then set out on the road to Piza. First got Irene's bike fixed and had a cup of milk and a bun.

Cycled 11 kilos and in the dark got put up on some straw in a farm in a small room next to a barn load of oxen. Slept warm and like tops.

02 October 1952 Thursday

The farm we were in was run by a very simple people. We cooked some tea in their kitchen. All they had to cook on was a fire on a raised slab in the corner. For breakfast a man there had bread in coffee and six sprats. Still we are on pretty near iron rations now and only have one good feed a day.

We cycled for about 40 kilos over quite pleasant open country, sometimes beside the sea, a few hills, but nothing much. Part of the way an Italian racing cyclist on practise kept us company. A few miles before Civitavechia we bought a loaf, some meat and chocolate spread, then sat on a bridge and ate the lot. I've never felt so hungry. Then we cycled on again. All the country consists of is ploughed land owned by the Italian Ministry of Agriculture. The air is fine and bracing and makes cycling easy. Numerous English cars pass us, the occupants don't look very happy, their only object being to get somewhere else. At Tarquinia, Irene got a puncture, it didn't take long to mend. Then we cycled on to Montalto-di-Castro and bought some food. A bit further on we made our supper by the road. Then in the moonlight moved to underneath a bridge that was once used to allow cattle through. That night the wind went through and we weren't warm and didn't sleep well.

03 October 1952 Friday

Woke up in a horrible mood, but breakfast eased it off a bit though we took time to move off. The countryside was much the same and really we had a pleasant day's cycle ride with nothing of any real note. The only thing is motor horns. Italian horns are usually higher pitched and loud. Also they use them at great length on the slightest provocation. Therefore two cyclists like us, loaded up with kit, cannot fail to bring forth a full quota of response, especially from the tiny little Fiats.

We were dog tired in the evening and the weather looked threatening. We asked at a Casa Cantoneira but they had no room. A few kilos further on we asked at a farm. A woman took us 100 yards to another little place and we were accommodated in a barn on some fresh cut planks of timber. Then we were invited upstairs to supper. That was a real good thing. There was a family of four. Two sons. The man did night work at some kind of mine. His wage was about 13/- a shift of eight hours.

Supper was very tasty and we enjoyed it. They don't eat much though. In spite of this we felt quite satisfied. The family are a little better off than those others we have met. They have a wireless and a motor cycle. They couldn't speak any English, but we managed to converse a bit, and I make them think I understand a lot more than I did. The trick is to repeat what they say to you but make it sound like a question. Slept well on the boards.

04 October 1952 Saturday

We were invited up to breakfast again in the morning. It consisted of bread soaked in coffee, followed by bread and cheese. Then as we were preparing to go they invited us to stay another day there. This was really wonderful. We got our washing done, bikes repaired and in general got sorted out. Besides having a good rest and good food all day. The family were extremely good and gave us lots to eat. In the evening we listened to the English news, then Irene and I had a little dance to the music on the wireless. The man was a Communist and didn't like the Pope. Among other things we learnt the rent was just over a pound a week, and that for three rooms and absolutely no conveniences.

05 October 1952 Sunday

Again bread and coffee for breakfast, however we finished this off with lots of bread and cheese and grapes, so felt fine. Irene wrote her letter home, and I messed around eating unripe quinces among other things. At 11.30 we were all ready to go. Then we really were struck by the kindness of the family. They gave us a loaf, cheese and grapes for dinner to take with us. Also stood at the door waving until we were out of sight.

It felt wonderful to be all set up and clean again. The break that family gave us was a real boon. We cycled a few kilos and stopped and ate all the food, then passed through the town of St. Vincenzo. There was a typical Sunday atmosphere, and lots and lots of young men dashing around on mini motors.

Late in the afternoon we reached Cecina. There was some form of celebration going on and there were lots of people about. We bought some food and then after some deliberation decided to go to Pisa on the main road via Leghorn. It soon got dark and we found ourselves cycling along over hilly country close to the sea. There were lots of houses about and the whole area looked like a popular residential district, with not much hope of finding a barn to sleep in. I enquired of a woman who spoke English and German, also at two houses, but we didn't get much help. Then a policeman stopped and asked us what we wanted. We told him and he asked a fellow passing if he had a place for us. We were taken up a hill and given a nice room to sleep in. It belonged to the fellow who had brought us. He worked as chauffeur to an American colonel who lived there, but the col. Was away, so we were fixed up. Irene had a bed and I on the floor. The fellow brought us honey sandwiches for supper.

06 October 1952 Monday

Got up about 8 and were given some really huge grapes for breakfast. Left at nine and after a short ride made some breakfast in a small wood. It wasn't a success though as our margarine had gone rank. Cycled on quite slowly to Leghorn. The sea looked beautiful, just what you expect of the Med. Leghorn looked a very nice town and we noticed the people looked far better off than in the south. There were a good many factories about. Left on the road to Pisa past a huge American depot of some sort. Half way to Pisa we stopped and cooked a meal. A couple of Scottish lads cycling from Lourdes to Rome stopped by and we had a pleasant talk. Got to Pisa about 5. Again no mail at the post. We seem to keep getting ahead all the time. Pisa struck us as being a very pleasant town, and the Leaning Tower was one of the tourist sights that came up to expectations. We saw it in the dusk.

Cycled again towards La Spezia and after one failure got a barn to sleep in. The floor was very hard.

07 October 1952 Tuesday

Up early, washed and a way. It was rather a dirty farm. Cooked the last of our soup and ate it with bread for breakfast then, a little further on, busted out and had six jam buns and a pint of milk each. After that cycled very slowly to Lerici. The country was getting a bit more mountainous and we passed lots of quarries. Also there were orange trees and some other yellowish fruit we didn't know.

Got to Lerici about 2 and after a long struggle got our bikes and ourselves up to the castle where the hostel is. It is a fine place. Comfortable and with cooking facilities. We could spend all day on top of the castle looking at the view around. Spent the rest of the evening buying and cooking a huge meal. Then, last thing at night, we danced to music on the radio. Two Germans were also out with a couple of Australian girls. The hostel is run by a queer woman who kept kissing the German lads. They all call her Madi. She runs the hostel well.

08 October 1952 Wednesday

Very easy day. Didn't do much at all except mend a puncture. Spent the morning in the sun on the roof. Spaghetti for dinner, though Irene got annoyed about something and didn't have any. In the afternoon we sat on the beach, I had a swim. Evening we cooked again. Very pleasant day.

09 October 1952 Thursday

We had to sit on the roof for nearly three hours waiting for Madi to come so that we could pay the bill. It was a beautiful day so we didn't mind waiting. Left the castle about 12 and sat on a seat in the town to eat lunch. Tried a fruit called Kaki. It was delicious. Passed through La Spezia and started walking uphill on the road to Genoa. By the time we had walked 4 kilos we saw no sign of reaching the top. We were lucky, and got a lift on the back of an empty truck. It took us 40 kilos over very hilly country and finally dropped us at the top of a mountain about 2,000 feet high. It was quite cold there. We cycled upwards just a little more and climbed to a vantage point above a restaurant which had flags of many nationalities outside it. Then we started going down, and halfway Irene's back inner tube burst. Changed it after a lot of cursing and messing about. By the time we reached the bottom we were freezing cold, and changed into pullovers trousers and gloves.

Decided to stay in the hostel at Chiavari, and after a lot of enquiries found it ok. There were only two Swiss lads there. Made a meal of pasta, tomatoes and onions, then went to bed.

10 October 1952 Friday

Woke up feeling tired and weak, so put it down to lack of nourishment and went out and bought a huge pile of food for breakfast. It took a long while to cook and a short while to eat, but we felt a lot better afterwards. Had a good wash and general sort out, and left the hostel about 12. Went to the market place and bought some apples. In the bank Irene met a man from Mancheser, he couldn't tell her what won the St. Leger though.

The road from Chiavari to Genoa is all hills and most hard work for cyclists. Also these little Rivierra hamlets by the coast with their numerous bars and hotels annoy us by their servility to the idle rich. Talked to a Scottish couple, Tulyar won the St. Leger. Arrived in Genoa towards evening. We were impressed by the town. It was much larger, cleaner and brighter, than we expected, and far above either Rome or Venice. Cycling through was most hectic. A young fellow told us of a camping place, but after much searching, we found the hostel. Dumped our kit there and went out. We walked along the waterfront and through a bazaar at the back. The sight of all the food made us hungry so we bought bones and spaghetti and came back and made a meal.

There was a very queer crowd in the hostel. Merchant seamen, American tourists and a few people that seem to exist for months on nothing. We talked with a very tall Englishman who had been 25 years in America. He was a bit of a boaster, but interesting. Then there was a young Englishman from Middlesbrough. He had been going for 11 weeks and hoped to remain till the end of November. An American woman travelling by car with daughter and husband was the worst character. She's enough to drive one to drink.

11 October 1952 Saturday

Sat up in bed and saw the oldish Australian we had met in Venice. He had been to Yugoslavia. Said the political influence was very strong and the people are wary of strangers. Went out shopping and had eaten my breakfast before Irene appeared. She made a tasty dish from kaki, milk and sugar. Left the hostel about 10. It was a long uncomfortable ride out of the city. The roads were terrible, one moment broad, the next narrow and always tram lines.

Eventually we left along the coast road. The sea looked beautiful and blue. The road kept fairly near to the coast though occasionally we went up a bit then there was a good view. Stopped in a small town for lunch, ate it sitting on a seat in the sun. Made ourselves overfull on bread and kaki. Got to Savonna about 3.30. Walked through the town centre. The streets are like cloisters and very cool and shady. Bought our evening meal there and left again. After going about 10 kilos we found a place with wood about, so we cooked our supper. Then as it grew dusk we went under the railway to a small open spot and pitched the tent.

12 October 1952 Sunday

Went about things very easy in the morning. Sat in the tent and had breakfast, and eventually got out about 9. Had a rinse in the sea and washed the dixies.

Made steady progress during the day, passing more little coastal resorts. We made quite a good lunch on 70 lire. Irene having bread and apple, and me bread and kaki. In the afternoon we were walking up a hill towards Imperia and got talking to an Englishwoman. She was most interesting. Invited us into a sort of station wagon in which she had been living for 16 years. She seemed to have been all over the world, and it must agree with her because she didn't look a bit like her 65 years. At first the conversation was about gigolos and the number of them around the area. We were told their best customers were Englishwomen. We were given tea and cakes and in all spent a most pleasant hour. When we left we were given half a pound of tea and a tin of cheese, plus two magazines. It was great help. We were also invited to write and perhaps meet again sometime.

After that we went through Imperia and out to a spot just before St. Lorenzo. We cooked supper, but were a bit worried as there were lots of lovers and odd characters about. Still when it was dark we found a spot and lay the beds down. An hour in bed and it started to rain, so the tent had to go up.

13 October 1952 Monday

Made a fire and cooked breakfast before leaving. Then a little way on had a good wash at a spring by the roadside. It must have looked queer to motorists passing. Got into San Remo about 12. Again no mail. We don't think much to the Italian postal service.

Cycled on a bit and had lunch sitting on a wall just out of the town. A very jovial character came up, shook hands, wished us well, and left. Stopped again in Bordeghera and spent the last of our lire. Bought biscuits, kaki and apples. I love Kaki Irene finds it sickly. Still mixed together in a mug with biscuits, and eaten with a spoon, it's delicious. After Ventimiglia we walked up a hill, down again, and up another very long one. Then we came to the border and passed through without the slightest trouble.

Didn't notice any real changes between France and Italy except that the people looked a little fairer and more prosperous. Cycled to Monte Carlo and Monaco. Walked down a street of shops akin to any English small town, then past the elaborate Sea Club, but perhaps it was because the place was out of season that we weren't impressed. Also it was raining and Irene adopted a 'very hard done by' attitude about it. Anyhow we left and headed for Nice.

NICE

Eventually got to Nice about 5.30 and were easily directed to a very nice little hostel on the third floor of a block of apartments. We lost no time in buying, cooking and eating a good meal. There were three north country English girls there and an English lad who had come to France with £5 in the hope of getting work. He had failed and was leaving that night to be repatriated at public experience. Tried to borrow 2 shillings - from us, failed.

The girls were out for a real good holiday. They had hitched around having spent a week in Paris, being taken out by various students. Their reminiscences were very frank and real eye openers to me.

14 October 1952 Tuesday

Left the hostel about 9.30. Walked around the market in Nice, bought food, then went out on the road to Cannes and cooked it. A policeman told us a fire was forbidden, but we could finish what we were doing and then make sure it was out. The wind blew hard against us and we had to struggle all the way to Cannes. It seemed a very nice town and I think the yachts in the harbour were the main interest. We were surprised at the number flying a British flag, also at the number of British cars in and about Cannes.

The hostel was on an island and the boat fare was too much. We were directed to La Bocea, 3 kms. away, but the hostel was closed there. A fellow from a hotel who spoke English showed us a filthy spot to camp, but we left and went back to Cannes.

Bought bread, and the people there gave us hot water. Previous to that I had been in the self-service section of a multiple store and spent 400 Francs. We made cocoa and ate bread and marg. Then cycled for about 5 miles in the dark on the road to Grasse. Found a field and pitched the tent.

15 October 1952 Wednesday

Lay awake a lot of the night, not cold or anything, but just sleepless. In the morning got everything packed and away, then we went out onto the road by a level crossing and cooked breakfast. Sat for an hour or so in the sun writing letters, then went on the way to Grasse. After about 4 kms. We started walking uphill. We walked through Grasse. The post office there hadn't change of 1000 Francs! Then on uphill towards Castellance. The scenery was magnificent. We stopped in a pleasant spot for dinner. Made a huge stew. Then carried on walking upwards. By about 6 we must have walked 12 kms. Went downhill for a mile to the village of St Vallier. It looked rather touristy, and I think I got a bad deal in a grocer's shop. It was dark after that, so we went a little way off the main road and made cocoa. Then pitched the tent.

I feel in poor shape. Constantly tired and nervy. I'm forever losing my temper and getting annoyed. Suppose it's money worry, and not enough food.

Still there's no need to worry, so must try and improve a bit.

16 October 1952 Thursday

Didn't rush about, got up about 7, cooked breakfast, washed in half a mug of water, wrote the log, pinched some quinces, fetched water, packed up and went. Walked uphill for 5 kms. Saw again the coast and Isle of St Margarita. The view was good, mountainous, but not overpoweringly so. After 5 kms. up we rode down again for 4 and stopped in a pleasant spot by a stream and cooked dinner. Also had a complete wash down. The going was not too bad after that and we intermittently rode and walked to Escrognolles. We had hoped to buy food there, but it was only a hamlet and no shops. Still we managed to buy bread, cheese and rice from the Auberge Napoleon. Cycled and walked some more through most beautiful country, and I really began to appreciate the beauty of Autumn. The colour of the trees was exquisite. We seemed to be going downhill a lot, passed along a lovely lonely valley, bounded by pine woods and mountains, and through the hamlet of Serancon. The valley opened out more with only hills at each side, the road became a little more civilized with restaurants and petrol stations. Then we went through some quiet pine woods, and as the sun was beginning to set, decided to camp. Went about 50 yards into the wood and found a good spot. Lit a fire and made cocoa, ate bread and cheese with it. Then when it was dark we put the tent up and made ourselves at home.

17 October 1952 Friday

Up at daybreak, lit a fire and had breakfast. Then spent over an hour mending punctures in Irene's bike. Also mended a hole in my pump connection, but it burst again.

Left the wood about 10. It was warm and in fact a beautiful day. The mountain country looked splendid in its autumn setting. We had quite an easy run for a few miles, then started to go up again so we stopped by a river and had a real delicate dinner. Boiled rice with milk and cheese, poured over a flapjack. It tasted excellent. Then for afters we had cocoa with bread soaked in it. Decided to have a quick wash, but Irene took a long time and got me annoyed., (My nerves at fault). Walked up the hill and then had a long run down into Castellane. It's a small town, and probably does well out of tourists. We bought some food there and then walked a good 5 miles uphill on the road to Dinge. It was evening when we got to the top, there were workmen there. Looked like Arabs. It was cold coming down the other side. We passed through a narrow and rugged gorge. Stopped at a farm and asked to sleep in the straw. Made supper there and went to bed. It wasn't comfortable as the straw was too soft and we gradually got buried into a tiny heap way under. Warm though!

18 October 1952 Saturday

Woke up early and dug my way upwards. Emerged into the cold air to find the ground covered in frost. Built a huge fire quickly and had bread and milk and fried bread. The sun rose over the mountains and we felt warmer. Packed the kit and left. Carried on cycling downhill. It was really cold and we stopped to put gloves on. It was a lovely morning and we had the same clear sky and beautiful autumn scenery.

Left on the road to Malejai and Grenoble and a short way up stopped and cooked dinner. One of the eggs we bought was bad, and the other broken so for dinner we had cheese, flapjack and potatoes, followed by boiled rice and figs. Had a wash after dinner and then cycled on for a couple of hours until evening. Bought bread at the village of Chateau Arnon and a short way out we had supper. Cycled in the dark for a while and asked at two farms to sleep in the barn. They refused. (Found out afterwards that owing to the Drummond murder they were forbidden to take in people like us). (At the moment Irene is cutting my hair, which accounts in part for occasional deviation of the pencil!). Went to a farm well back off the road and got put up excellently in a hay loft. It was very warm and comfortable, had electric light too.

19 October 1952 Sunday

As usual we both lay awake for a long while before dawn, but I was the one who enjoyed it. Irene wasn't so comfortable. At 5 o'clock the farmer came to feed the horses, and we got up shortly after. Got everything packed and had a sort of a wash. I asked if we could light a fire for breakfast, and they offered us the use of their kitchen. That was excellent. The kitchen was warm and we soon got our tea made. The people there also put a huge bowl of hot milk before us, and for once we made a really good breakfast. It's surprising what a difference bread with milk is as compared with bread and water. The family at the farm lived, I should imagine, much the same as an English farming family. Maybe their living standards are not quite so high, but I think they are fairly comparable. They consisted of the farmer and his wife, aged around 40. A daughter of 21 and a son of 7. Also Grandma and Grandpa. We never saw Grandma. The talk about continentals having a light breakfast didn't seem to fit too well here. There was a hunk of bacon, cheese and jam on the table, and the farmer ate liberal quantities of each, together with several glasses of wine and a bowl of coffee. We made do on a huge plate of bread and milk, tea and bread and marg. Also we were given some of the fig jam. The figs were whole so it could hardly be spread on bread, still it was good to taste.

It started to rain and everyone turned out to pull in a cart of pumpkins and in general get things under cover. I noticed here that the farmer's wife seemed to do a lot more outdoor work than the daughter. I think the daughter did most of the housekeeping. We thought it best not to leave in the rain, and I sat in the barn mending Irene's shoe. Then, when Irene had finished washing up in the kitchen, she came down with a mirror and scissors to cut her hair. The business ended with my neck getting shaved raw, and most of MY hair getting cut off. Irene made a most amateurish job of it and I was pretty peeved at the time. Still I've been peevish over many things just lately, so that was not unusual.

Left the farm at about 11. It was hard to part as they had a lovely chicken boiling on the stove, and oh how we could have tucked into that. Still there was no excuse to stay and we didn't get invited, so there was no help for it. (The farm was 12 miles from the scene of the Drummond Murders).

Cycled 6 kms to Sisteron, and bought some pressed meat for dinner. There was a fork in the road three kms. from the town, one going to Grenoble via Gap and the other, slightly shorter, via La Col de Croixe Harte. We decided on the shorter route. The road was quite deserted. The countryside most peaceful and pleasant. The weather was dull, but fitted the autumn colour, and in all made us feel quite happy. We sat by the road and ate the meat. It gave Irene indigestion made me run. Still, at the time it seemed a good meal. After dinner we cycled on into Sevres. The mountains seemed to close in on us then and at every turn we expected a huge hill. Still the road kept fairly flat through Aspres and Aspremont. And, apart from two occasions when I had to depart from the road in great haste and make for a hedge, we kept going at a slow pace, which didn't please me greatly.

Towards evening we left Aspres and headed up the road towards the Col. It was not difficult going and we made 5 miles to the village of La Laurie where I bought food. Cycled on some more for about 3 kms. Stopped near a barn and made supper. There were horses in the barn and I went there to investigate the chances of getting a kip there. Found that two grooms slept there with the horses. The inside of the barn looked much like a robbers' den, but I asked if we could sleep there. They said, yes, and cleared a space on the hard floor. We slept to the sound of 5 horses steadily masticating and occasionally snorting. Luckily their noisy urination ran into a drain which divided our hard bed-place from them. The grooms were Italians working in France. One had been there 6 years, the other 5. Neither had ever been back to Italy.

20 October 1952 Monday.

Lay for hours waiting for the light, got quite cold around the middle, then went to sleep and it got light, so we didn't get up as quickly as intended. Still, we were up pretty early. Packed everything and said goodbye to our hosts. Made a fire in a small wood and had breakfast. It began to rain a little, washed quickly in a stream and started off. The rain came in fits and starts and we wore gas capes. The road led upwards gradually and we still hadn't come to the long hill we expected to the Col.

Watched the kms. slip by until eventually there was only one more to the top and before us a long steady incline, with the railway beside it. We cycled up it with the wind behind us, and were most thankful for the ease of our ascent. Stopped a while and ate two figs each. Then down the other side. This was a different matter altogether. Zig Zag bends and steep slopes for about 8 kms. It made us realize we must have been climbing up the other side for days. The countryside was simply marvellous. The rain poured down and we got soaked, but we didn't mind, the weather so fitted the surroundings. We have never seen such colouring.

There were several little clustered villages below us, all looking so peaceful and permanent, and no sign of council house extensions that are the vogue in England. Stopped and picked apples and later pears. Also tried for a lift, as we were still 60 kms. From Grenoble. A surly driver told us to go to the station and catch a train.

It was too cold to stop and we kept going occasionally uphill, but - over a Bailey Bridge - and more often down and the whole experience was an enjoyment. Then a long hill and we reached the township of St Agnon-en Monestier. Stopped there for a quick lunch of bread and cheese. Grenoble still 35 kms. away.

We thought we had just about reached the limit of descent, but we didn't start pedalling again until 17 kms from Monestier, and we did that in less than 20 minutes. We passed the village where road repairs were going on. The weather got colder, but the rain stopped. Irene got off to walk as the road frightened her, and as usual I got impatient. The ride then into Grenoble was uneventful and not very interesting. We arrived about 3 having done nearly 60 miles in less than 5 hours. (Discovered later 4 broken spokes in my back wheel).

Went to the post, there was a letter for Irene and none for me. Enquired of several people for the hostel and eventually got there. It was in a back alley up a flight of stairs with a squat lavatory at their foot. I went up first to get the gen. There was one room with a lot of mattresses on the floor. A young girl lay on one, covered in a blanket. A group of people were around a table-tennis table. They looked at first a very queer crowd, intellectuals of some sort, long hair and beards etc. I asked about the hostel and it seemed quite good. There was gas, bed and water, and the cost 60 francs a night.

We have got used to dossing now, and the fact that everyone lives together in one room didn't worry us a bit. We soon got settled in, and had a cup of tea. Then some food, and then a big meal. Cheese, rice and a flapjack. We had plenty to do in the way of washing clothes etc., and spent the evening doing that.

Didn't quite know what to make of our companions at first. Only one spoke English and he went to bed early. One of the young girls was seriously smoking a pipe. Then people began to drift in. Some played table tennis. It was quite a friendly atmosphere. A new entrant usually went around to everyone, shook hands and said 'salut' A dark young fellow sat beside me and started speaking excellent English. I learnt he was an Algerian working in France. He told me many things about the people there, and what I had suspected as being a very Bohemian hide out changed into a simple case of several young people looking for work, and living as cheaply as possible until they found it.

My friend was very helpful when I told him we would like to get work, and he made several suggestions, and explained things a bit. Still, it looked as if we would have had to wait about two or more weeks for a job, and our money just wouldn't run to that. We sat up quite late eating boiled chestnuts.

21 October 1952 Tuesday

Grenoble - Paris

Woke up early as usual and the anticipated enjoyment of having a long lie in bed did not really materialise. Still we had a very easy and pleasant morning, not finishing breakfast until 11. Went out for a walk around Grenoble, but it was lunch hour and most of the shops were shut. Grenoble does not seem to be an extra large town, though it is larger than average. We were wearing plimsolls as our shoes were still wet, and it made walking difficult, so we soon went back to the hostel and had a meal. I spent four hours trying to put four new spokes in my wheel, then discovered they were too short, so took it to a repair shop. Spent the rest of the evening reading. Irene cooked dinner and we had a big meal of cauliflower, potatoes and cheese sauce.

22 October 1952 Wednesday

Getting up was a bit harder, but we made it ok. Spent the morning and 230 francs getting the bikes in order. Used olive oil to cook dinner, but it tasted too sickly for me. Irene liked it.

Sat for a long while talking about vitality. Afternoon, played table tennis, then had a wash and went out. Walked around the shops, they stay open till after 7 pm. Enquired at the station the cost of the train to Paris. It was too much. It rained so back to the hostel. I have been surprised at the apparent aimlessness in living of the people we have seen here. They don't seem to get any enjoyment out of life, and are just content to carry on from day to day, working, eating, sleeping. The young people in the hostel here, all between about 18 and 25, an age when everything should be vital, and have an object, are living more or less from hand to mouth. They lounge around most of the time in this one room, eating very little, talking, I can't understand it, never do I hear their voices raised in anger, excitement or hilarity. They seem spiritless, and indeed to live for weeks under such conditions must bring out signs of impatience in the most phlegmatic of individuals. Yet in these I see none. They are most difficult to understand, I can't imagine similar situations among the young English soldiers I had recently served with. Another queer thing about the hostel is the spirit of comradeship and share and share alike. Somebody must buy the fuel, though I don't know who. Somebody buys food, but anyone seems to eat it. Also there are quite a lot of valuable oddments lying around and a box of money on the table. It says something for the trustfulness of whoever organises this mysterious society.

In the evening a group of young people came in for some sort of meeting. There seemed to be little organisation, but they were all bright and gay. First talking then singing then old fashioned dancing. Even so it still seemed pretty pointless and no object. A fellow who spoke English talked with us for a while. Played table tennis at about 11, then went to bed. A group of five or so were still sitting together changing numerous extremely doleful melodies.

23 October 1952 Thursday

PARIS AND HOME

Up early, cooked breakfast and prepared to go. Then it started to rain and we messed about till 11.

Thought maybe we'd get away without paying, as nobody seemed to care whether we did or not, but at the last moment we had to fill in a book and hand over 390 francs. Left with our feet wrapped up in sacks to keep the rain out. Felt much off form after our long rest but the hilly country between Voiron and Les Albrets cured us, though at one spot Irene had a little breakdown.

The rain kept coming and going all the day, but only our feet got wet and cold. Found ourselves on the road to Bourg for a bit after dark, then asked at a farm to sleep. The welcome was spontaneous and absolutely good-hearted and cheerful. A happy healthy looking man about 40 years old in blue overalls ran the farm with wife, auntie and six children. We were invited into the house to eat and given goat's cheese and wine. One of the boys looked like a scholar and spent his time doing geometry. It looked incongruous in such surrounding. We had a warm bed on the straw.

24 October 1952 Friday

Lay in till 8 o'clock, it was so comfortable. Got up then and the cheerful farmer shook hands and asked us 'bien dormier?' several times. Had a good wash in a tub they lent us and then we were invited in to cook breakfast. Made a nice dish of porridge and ate it with bread and milk. Auntie and the wife were cutting up a huge dish of apples for jam. They gave us a piece of sweet made from quince. It tasted much of figs. When we left we paid for the milk and two cheeses made from goats' milk.

It was 10 am. The family were just sitting down to a meal of bread and soup. The weather was dull but not wet and we had quite an uneventful ride to Bourg. Ate dinner (bread and cheese) at a village where the road crosses the Rhone. An old woman gave us hot water for cocoa. Then in the evening we sat on a seat just outside Bourg and had tea. It seems a good idea this asking for hot water. Cycled on in the dark towards Chalon, and an excitable motorist stopped to tell Irene she must have lights. Tried at two farms for a place to sleep, but no luck. At the third we got accommodated nicely in the hay barn of a small farm. The farmer was fairly young, with seven children and another on the way.

25 October 1952 Saturday

Sat in the barn and ate breakfast, they gave us just a little hot water and we made tea. It was raining, so we tied our ankles up well with sacks, and set off. The farm we left was a dirty place, I believe the cattle were not healthy. The lavatory was extremely primitive. Yet they were good to us, and we felt sorry for them.

We kept going very well in spite of the rain and did the 64 kms to Chalon in 3 and a half hours. Then got some hot water at a baker's near the centre and had a meal there. Left Chalon about 2 pm and soon got to Chagny. Noticed a complete change in the type of town. It seemed more like any English small town in an industrial region. We were feeling tired but kept going slowly and got up and over one of the last big hills we hope to encounter. Bought food at Ivry en Montagne and then cycled on more. It was dark and we got pulled up by a police patrol because Irene had no light. After a lot of "I do not understand" on both sides they just us gave up as a bad job and left. There was some terribly bad road repairing and we had to walk. Before that we had been to a house and asked to sleep. The man was very kind and gave us three addresses to go to. Still it would have meant going back a bit, so we decided to carry on.

While walking over the bad road we came to a farm and got put up. Then went into the kitchen and had cocoa, milk and tea. Very warm and comfortable. Happy family of 8, seemed not too badly off. Slept well and warm. Conscience pricked me a bit though. Hope we have not carried disease from the dirty farm of last night. Still, I should imagine if it was anything serious they would have taken more precautions.

26 October 1952 Sunday

Another warm and good night's rest. Up about 8, washed and had cocoa and milk in the farm. The weather was fine and we set off for Arnay le Duc. We had been told that the train fare to Paris was 1000 francs and, at that rate, we should have saved money in getting there. However at the station we were told the fare was 1600 francs and that was a bit too much. Spent the next two hours outside a cycle shop putting in new spokes. Three more had gone from my back wheel. Left about 12, and then stopped again after a few kms for dinner. It rained a bit, but we ate a good meal standing up.

Arrived at Sanlier about 3 and passed onto the road to Avallon. There were quite a few hills, and in one place the road was being repaired. They had made a terrible mess of the place. Got to within 18 kms of Avallon and then we were diverted up a side turning. Seems they'd closed off a whole section of road to repair it. Still, we didn't mind as we were on a pleasant country lane. Cycled on till dusk then asked at a farm. It was a large place. The farmer appeared to live there along with wife and son. He was rather quiet, and wanted to see our passports. Still, we got on quite well, gave me a glass of wine and we had a nice pile of straw in the cleanest barn yet, so felt well satisfied. Ate bread and figs for supper. It was a bit disconcerting to know that after cycling for over an hour we were still 18 kms from Avallon though.

27 October 1952 Monday

We were asked in for a breakfast of coffee and bread. There was lots of milk and we made a good meal. There were two of the farm hands there together with the farmer. They had a meal of bread and milk followed by cheese and coffee. Actually we thought our host and his wife a rather queer pair. Very subdued and careful though I should imagine they were quite well off. I never felt such hard work-worn hands as the woman had when we shook hands goodbye. There was frost and a very cold nip in the air. It was about 7.30 when we left and the sun had not risen. Cycled about 400 yards then stopped and put on long trousers and wrapped my hands in sacking. The pair of gloves I found at Zell also proved most welcome. We decided not to follow the road diversion through to Avallon, but to cut off a corner by going along minor roads. This would save us about 8 kms. and bring us out on the main road at Vermonton, halfway between Avalon and Auxerne. This we did, and even though at times the road was a mere track, we had a really pleasant hour and a half ride in the clear crisp morning air, over quiet rolling hills and through a couple of out of the way villages. We were warm and hungry at Vermonton and also the carrier on my bike needed mending, so we stopped, ate bread and figs, and fixed it.

The R6 highway was simply perfect, miles and miles of smooth tarmac, we sailed along in great style. Through Auxerne, which looked a pleasant town rather like Cambridge, and on to Joigny. Since last night I had been looking forward to sardines for dinner as a change from the usual cheese. We sat on a seat in the sun at Joigny with a cup of cocoa and the sardines, and really enjoyed ourselves.

Kept going after that for another 20 kms, and at one point where we stopped for something or other, three consecutive trucks pulled up when we signalled them for a lift. Two weren't going far, the third would have taken us to Paris if we had given him money. I did not feel it would have been worth while travelling in such company. Later Irene's new back tube, that I had bought yesterday, developed a puncture. Halfway through mending it a lorry stopped and a pleasant young man offered us a lift to Sens. So we piled the bikes in and I sat in the back and had the punctures (two of them) mended by the time we arrived. Kept on cycling then and when we were 80 kms from Paris (having done 145 in a day, (a record for us, as we cycled 125 of them) we called it a day. Went to a farm, got hot milk and was accommodated in a dutch barn. Made a most excellent bed up near the roof, on and in between, hay bales.

28 October 1952 Tuesday

Bought milk and eggs at the farm and they were kind enough to cook it for us and let us eat in their kitchen. We also got a good wash there, and were off on the road by 7.30. Thought how different that farm was compared with some we have been in. Really though, there was a bit too much organisation for my liking.

Felt tired after yesterday's long ride. Stopped a bit after 5 kms and loaded up with lots of apples. Finished off another 35 kms and went past SHAEF HQ I think, and through the Forest of Fontainbleau until we were about 39 Kms from Paris. Then our luck was in and we got a lift in a small van. He took us about 30 Kms. It was only running on two cylinders when we got in, and when we left it, it had seized up altogether. I offered to wait while the driver telephoned, but he seemed quite at ease, so we left. The next three hours were quite hectic. Cycling around in Paris. First we made enquiries at the Gare du Nord about trains and boats home. And then were delighted to find three letters waiting for us at the post. Sat in the Jardin de Tuilleries and ate bread and figs. Also talked to a melancholy American until 4.45. He seemed quite a nice fellow, and then suddenly started quoting the comparative prices of street women here and in Germany. It rather shocked us, but we were about to leave anyway, so said goodbye.

Thought I'd found the hostel site and that it had been pulled down, had a few anxious moments, but a woman put us right. Got there, had a good wash down and a meal, then spent the rest of the evening listening and occasionally arguing (though it was difficult to get a word in) with a fluent, interesting and extremely effervescent Dutchman who, apart from visiting the Olympic Games at Helsinki, had been working his way around the continent for four months with an English girl. I slept in a tent to save money.

29 October 1952 Wednesday

Irene brought me tea in bed. Cooked herrings for breakfast and thoroughly enjoyed it. Left the hostel about 10.30 and after a long walk reached the Eiffel Tower. Irene went up and was thrilled by it. It would have been nice to go up together, but I had been up before so sat at the bottom, wrote the log, and listened to numerous American tourists talking. They seemed to outnumber the French by far at that particular spot.

From the Eiffel Tower we walked to the Place d'Etoile and sat there and had our lunch. It rained a little, so we weren't comfortable. Walked down the Champs Elysee and spent 20 minutes or so looking around a dog shop. I think that was the most enjoyable. Got to the post about 4.30 and found a letter for each of us. Of all things Colin has got married.

Felt there had been something worrying them at home, but now I am glad it's all over. Walked along the Rue Rivoli and the banks of the Seine looking at the 'Art' for sale there. We criticised the serious art like a couple of connoisseurs and pronounced it trash, but we enjoyed the funny and witty. Irene's foot was hurting, so forked out 60 francs for two metro tickets (that was what I had made by taking two milk bottles back earlier). Before that though we had bought some mince meat and margarine at a shopping centre by the Blvd. St Germain.

Got back to the hostel and made a fine dish of spaghetti. The Dutchman we had spent yesterday evening talking was there in a state of unusual dejection. He was flat broke and only had some porridge to cook for his girl friend, who was expected home from work about 7. She came in shortly, having worked at sewing from 8.30 until 6.30 with one and a half hours for lunch, but absolutely nothing to eat or drink all that time. Seems like they see the world the hard way.

About 8 pm I went off with the Dutchman and an Australian to look for work unloading trucks at les Halles. First, however, the other two were off to the Place Pigalle to see the 'gay life of Paris.' Actually we spent two hours or so walking past gaudy cafes and caberets with 'saucy' window displays, and looking at the numerous street women to be seen there.

Left the Australian then and went to Les Halles. There were quite a few trucks there, but lots and lots of helpers. We got talking (or rather the Dutchman did, he's rather a linguist) to two oldish fellows who tried to help us, but at midnight we caught a tube back. It seemed that not many trucks come in on a Wednesday, so tomorrow night we go again and meet the same two fellows, they offered us coffee, and promised a supper if we didn't get work tomorrow. On the tube met an American married couple saying at the hostel, and as usual, the Dutchman talked animatedly all the way home. Outside the Porte d'Orleans station three girls rushed up, said they had heard the Dutchman talking on the train and wondered what nationality he was. They were Americans staying for a year in Paris. We talked for 20 minutes, then back to the hostel and bed.

30 October 1952 Thursday

Went to the Louvre and was greatly impressed by the Mona Lisa. It really is a masterpiece. Also saw a great deal of the priceless art treasures, but by 2 pm we had had enough. Sat on a window ledge, ate lunch then went to the post office and wrote home.

Irene got a bit miserable on the way back home and we had a serious talk. Don't know really what the outcome will be. Things were quite agreeable by the time we got back to the hostel. Spent the evening talking, mainly with a young American married couple.

Three of us went to Les Halles and got work. Worked for about 3 hours and got paid for 6, at the rate of 100 francs an hour. Staggered back to the hostel with the Dutch lad at 6 am. My whole body ached. The job was unloading fruit and vegetables. Felt annoyed to see young Americans wasting money. To me now its value represents sleep and labour. Actually the money I earned from night work in Les Halles was the cost of Irene's trip to the top of the Eiffel Tower, and my reward was to have this lovely young girl from Millbrook leaning over the upper balcony and waving to me 1000 feet below.

31 October 1952 Friday

Walked back to hostel and went to bed in the tent. Irene brought me tea at 8, but I stayed in bed till 4 pm, and even then felt tired. Irene spent the day with the Dutchman's girlfriend. They got on well together. I had a good wash down and spent the evening as usual at the hostel. The Dutchman was a magnificent entertainer on the guitar and we had a really enjoyable evening.

Set off for Les Halles at 10.50. There were five of us this time. A Dutchman, Swiss, Italian, Australian and myself. However we were unlucky as they would only take people with an insurance card. Wandered around with the Dutchman a while and earned a cauliflower, then we picked up fruit and vegetables that had been dropped, and got back about 2.30 am.

01 November 1952 Saturday

Irene brought me a cup of tea in bed, and then I got up washed, and had breakfast. Spent some time darning my socks, then we gathered up several milk bottles and took them back to the shop and got money on them. One woman wanted to know when we were going to buy milk. Pete, a Swiss lad who had hitch-hiked to the Sudan and back, came with us for the day. It was raining so we took a metro to the Gare du Nord. Enquired some more about fares home. Walked around Place Pigalle, went to the youth hostel in Rue Victor Mare, but there was only time to use the toilet before it closed. Sat in an archway and ate banana sandwiches. Another American couple wanted to know where they could leave their bags. Suddenly remembered had to get a traveller's cheque cashed. But everything seems closed in Paris on a Saturday afternoon. However a fellow at the American Express office advised us to go to Grand Hotel. Then we spent an hour at the post office writing. Then made our way by metro back to the hostel.

There weren't so many there that evening. Made a sort of cheese stew for supper and shared it with an Italian. A fellow put on a wireless, but none of us liked it as it disrupted conversation. Listened to the Dutchman's guitar, then bed.

02 November 1952 Sunday

Decided to cycle around today. Arranged tickets for the train tomorrow morning, and found ourselves left with about 500 francs. Visited the Invalides and Court of Napoleon, but didn't fancy paying 80 francs to go in. Cycled down the Champs Elysee and climbed the Arc de Triumph. Bought mayonnaise and bread for lunch and had it somewhere near the Bastille. Went to Notre Dame, but it wasn't very impressive. That's not all in the right order, but the facts are there. Rode along the banks of the river looking at the various art vendors' wares. Some of it is filthy.

Usual evening in hostel, though I had to clean up last thing. Put all the spare food in the part belonging to the flat broke Dutchman.

03 November 1952 Monday

Didn't hear the alarm, but got up and away ok. Had plenty of time before the train left. Uneventful 4 hour journey to Calais. There we met a theological student who had been studying in Switzerland for 18 months. He treated us to a first class lunch in the restaurant. Also talked a bit with an oldish American couple. The crossing was rough, but not unpleasant. It was good to get real value for my last 100 francs. Bought 3 teas and 3 cakes. The boat was very empty. Got through the customs and just laughed when he asked what we had to declare. Promptly set off on the right hand side of the road.

Dear Aunt Flo, who lives near Dover, gave us a fine supper, and plied us with questions.

It was lovely.

THE END

Olivio and Agostina – who we stayed with in their home near Grosseto for two nights. They sent a lovely letter with a Spaghetti recipe, which I still have.

Olivio and Agostina's sons, Felinolo, Ovarro and Claude

Irene looking over Symonds Yat – Mount Snowden – Trial run before tackling bike trip through Europe

Hans and Irene picnicking on the way from Rottenburg to Augsberg

Youth Hostel at Rottenburg

On route from Rottenburg to Augsberg

On route from Rottenburg to Augsberg

Me and Hans in Nordlingen

Italian family we met in Northern Italy

Irene with all the children and Peter & Joy Amis - Pete was my best friend from childhood and best man at our wedding

Irene with John, our first born, one year after our return from Europe

Me and Irene on a walk in the country 1954

Irene with John and Adrian

Left to Right: Irene's father Jo Powell, Auntie Kitty our landlady in our first proper home, Irene's mum Olive, my brother in laws Mum, my Mum Kitty Brown, Tina and Colin, my brother and his wife. Children left to right: Andrew, Adrian, John, my brother's children Sally Anne, Billy and Colin junior.

Irene 1953 visiting London to meet Hans

Before setting off on a trial run to Mount Snowden 1952

Irene with John, Andrew, Kathy, Joanna and Adrian (Joe)

With Han's wife Annaleise at Broughton House.

EPILOGUE.

I hope you have found the Diary interesting, and will think of us if you ever find yourself visiting some of the places mentioned in it.

I think the roots of our travels lie way back in 1939 when the war broke out.

In 1939 I watched the barrage balloons flying over Alexandra Palace in North London. I was also awarded a place at Southgate County Grammar School. In 1940 I spent a week there and then left the Spitfires and Hurricanes flying over the Alley Pally and Mother took us to live with her country cousins near Cambridge. I attended Sawston Village College for the next three years and had an excellent grounding in metal and wood work, and a rudimentary grounding in the three R's and not much else.

By the age of 17 all I wanted was to join the army and go abroad. A little later I went to Maidstone and took the King's shilling and signed on in the Royal Armoured Corps. It was 1946 when I waved a fond farewell to my parents and younger brother Colin. The war was over, and for six years I had a great time in Germany, Italy, Austria, Egypt, Libya and Cyprus. I became an instructor in driving and maintenance of tanks and armoured cars, but also during the long periods of static duty in the Middle East I began to do something about my education.

By the time I left the army I had gained 5 A level passes in the Forces Preliminary Examination - a wartime measure to help servicemen who's education had been disrupted by the war. It was geared to gain exemption from London Matriculation, but I did not know its value at that time, and instead took a job as trainee manager in a large chain store group

Irene and I on our wedding day

Meanwhile Irene was born in Plymouth in 1932 the only daughter (following 3 sons) of Joe and Olive Powell. Her parents were from Roche, St Austell in Cornwall. The Hamlet of Woon where Joe Powell grew up is now buried under the china clay waste heaps.

Irene spent her early years in Millbrook where she had an ideal childhood disrupted by the war during which time her Father Joe was conscripted into the Navy as a Ships tailor.

She attended Saltash Grammar school and when we met was working as a Hotel Receptionist in Southend on Sea. She and her friend Kate decided at the last minute to go to the Kursaal dance that New Years Eve and I'm eternally grateful they did!

In 1953 Irene and I married and by 1962 I was assistant manager in the Birmingham store. By 1965 we'd bought our first home, Broughton House in Drakes Broughton, Worcestershire, and five lovely children. It was a happy home life. Irene was a kind and loving Wife and Mother who loved singing and making up stories for our children. We both had our roles, and the trials and tribulations we overcame during our three month bike trip played a big part in making our marriage a successful one.

After our youngest child started school, Irene, a talented writer and story teller was offered a job with the Berrows Worcester Journal, writing a childrens page. It was a huge success and for 10 years Irene was a bit of a local celebrity known as Aunty Renee . The children's page was full of stories, poetry and competitions, I still have all the press cuttings and stories and tapes from that time.

Twenty three years later the children had left home and Irene and I were partners in a successful insurance brokerage. Then I could afford to do something I had long wanted to do. While Irene remained in the business I went to teacher training college.

Five years later I was Head of Business Studies in a Huntingdon Comprehensive. I should have become a teacher long ago. I loved it. A Secondary Modern Education, six years in the army and a beautiful wife who had stuck with me through thick and thin. Five kids in 9 years. Life as a father and businessman, the experience of self-employment and business life. I was ready for those comprehensive school children who had been treated as no hopers.

I loved teaching. I loved those kids. Right from the start we identified with each other.

Our wedding day 9th May 1953

In 1986 Irene and I went on a Commonwealth Teacher Exchange to Australia . We exchanged job, house, car with an Australian teacher for a year. On return I was offered early retirement and VSO

(Voluntary Service Overseas) had shown interest in sending Irene and I as aid workers in the Highlands of Papua New Guinea. On return we went to work for Eurocamp in France and Italy for several wonderful seasons. We had a great time.

In January 2002 Irene was diagnosed with dementia and I was her 24/7 carer until she passed away unexpectedly on January 15th 2010. She is the inspiration behind publishing this book and remains the Love of my Life.

Acknowledgements

As I read again the diary of our journey, it feels like yesterday, the memories are so clear. The rich experience of our travels - although it didn't always seem rich - was the experience we shared and the wonderful people we met. We experienced the kindness of many simple people along the back roads of Belgium, Holland, Germany, Austria, Italy, and France.

We didn't always note down names but the people and places mentioned here have always had a place in our hearts.

The Van Loom family in Holland who gave us shelter during a storm just after Irene was knocked off her bike by a runaway dog. We had a lovely day and night with them, and some of the best coffee we have ever tasted.

Hans Mueller who we met at the Youth Hostel in Rhotenbourg ab Tauber, and spent three days with him cycling from Rhotenbourg to Augsburg. We and our families remain close friends even after all these years.

The level crossing keeper in the dark Austrian Alps, who allowed us to stay the night in his railway hut when the gloomy mountains looked dark and threatening.

The Cafe by the Ponto Rialto in Venice where we had been recommended for a low cost meal.

The roadside farm near Mestre where we were allowed to cook in their kitchen, and Irene was warned that Mama would not like to see her wearing shorts.

The truck drivers who gave us an overnight lift to Foggia and allowed Irene to sleep on one of the bunks behind the seat and the two drivers who kept that truck on the move throughout the night.

The people at the gas station in Foggia who insisted we wait while they got us a lift to Naples over the Bandit filled mountains to Naples. And the five men in the cab who bought us a lovely meal at a mountain roadside cafe.

The people on the road to Rome who allowed us to bed down for the night after Irene had caught her wheel in a railway crossing and fallen off her bike.

The people in a Farm on the outskirts of Rome who allowed us to bed down in their barn while the smoke from their cooking fire drifted through a hole in the roof.

The policeman on the road near Leghorn who arranged for us to sleep in an empty holiday home and the owner who bought us a huge bunch of grapes for breakfast.
The young family near Grosseto who allowed us to sleep in their barn, gave us supper, and then invited us to stay another day to allow us to do washing,

and get ourselves back in order. Later she sent us a letter with her instructions for making spaghetti.

The 65 year old lady near Cannes who had been living in her station wagon for 16 years and just returned from Corsica and invited us to join her for tea and cakes.

Fond memories of kind people and wonderful places.

Personal Acknowledgements

My thanks to my darling wife Irene for giving me the happiest years of my life.

To Hans Muller and his family for the wonderful years of friendship.

To our children, John, Joe, Andrew, Joanna and Kathy for their love and support.

Special thanks to Kathy for her hard work and help in getting this book finished.

Also special thanks to my brother Colin, his wife Val, my cousin Doreen, my lifelong friend Pete Amis (R.I.P) and his wife Joy, for their love and support.

And thanks to all the wonderful people we've met throughout the years who have helped to make our lives so rich.